Thanks to Erwin Lutzer for dropping this bomb on the pure fabrication of *The Da Vinci Code*. The heresies of second- and third-century Gnosticism are alive and well. May this book put those heresies to rest in our time.

DR. R. C. SPROUL
CHAIRMAN AND FOUNDER, LIGONIER MINISTRIES

Erwin Lutzer provides a timely answer for those who are tempted to place their faith on the shifting sands of popular culture rather than the solid rock of God's unchanging truth. *The Da Vinci Deception* will help you navigate through the claims of a culture that has abandoned the true Jesus for an image made in its own likeness.

THOMAS H. L. CORNMAN, PhD
CHURCH HISTORIAN
VICE PRESIDENT AND DEAN OF THE UNDERGRADUATE SCHOOL
MOODY BIBLE INSTITUTE

Dr. Lutzer has done it again. When it comes to making clear the moral and philosophical confusion of our day, no one does it better. His analysis of *The Da Vinci Code* is thorough, insightful, and convincing.

SANDY RIOS
PRESIDENT, CULTURE CAMPAIGN

If Lutzer writes it, I read it. He is a scholarly pastor and a dynamic preacher and author who connects with the culture and offers clear and compelling evidence for truth. He enables the reader to separate truth from fiction, fact from fantasy, and reality from myth. *The Da Vinci Deception* is a must read. It cracks the codes of conspiracy and enables us to believe with confidence in "the faith once delivered."

DR. JACK GRAHAM
PRESIDENT, SOUTHERN BAPTIST CONVENTION
PASTOR, PRESTONWOOD BAPTIST CHURCH, PLANO, TEXAS

THE DA VINCI DECEPTION

THE DA VINCI DECEPTION

ERWIN W. LUTZER

Living
Books®

TYNDALE HOUSE PUBLISHERS, INC., CAROL STREAM, ILLINOIS

Visit Tyndale's exciting Web site at www.tyndale.com

TYNDALE is a registered trademark of Tyndale House Publishers, Inc.

Tyndale's quill logo is a registered trademark of Tyndale House
Publishers, Inc.

Living Books is a registered trademark of Tyndale House Publishers, Inc.

First printing of Living Books edition February 2006

The Da Vinci Deception

Designed by Luke Daab

ISBN-13: 978-1-4143-0633-9
ISBN-10: 1-4143-0633-4

Printed in the United States of America

10 09 08 07 06
 8   7

*To our good friends
David and Nancy Lagerfeldt,
who alerted me to the fact
that some people reading
The Da Vinci Code were
confusing legends with facts
and superstitions with sober
history. Your commitment to
the authentic Jesus has
helped others find the way.*

TABLE OF CONTENTS

TABLE OF *DA VINCI CODE* FREQUENTLY ASKED QUESTIONS

Who do you say that I am?"

The disciples knew what others were saying about Jesus. Some thought that he was John the Baptist or one of the prophets—but Jesus wanted a personal response: "Who do *you* say that I am?"

Jesus pressed for their answer, not about what he was saying or doing; he did not ask whether the disciples liked him or not. His question went to the heart of who he was as a person. Was he just an extraordinary man, or was he something more?

Even today the question still haunts us.

The controversy that surrounded the release of the movie *The Passion of The Christ* proved that this question still cries for an answer. Justin Pope, in a recent *Chicago Sun-Times* article, says that Jesus is a distant symbol with many interpretations. "There's black Jesus, and white Jesus. Homely and handsome, capitalist and socialist, stern and hippie. Hardworking social reformer, mystical comforter."[1]

The Da Vinci Code offers a different answer: Jesus the married man; Jesus the feminist; Jesus the mortal prophet. It's clear that everyone has an opinion about Jesus.

In this book, we'll investigate the historical roots of early Christianity. We'll seek to give credible answers to these questions: Who is Jesus? Are the documents of the New Testament reliable accounts of his life and ministry? And what should this mean to us who live in the twenty-first century?

We'll take a look at how dissenters of the early centuries offered their own radical interpretation of the life and mission of Jesus. These dissenters had their own documents, their own religious convictions, and their own teachers. In this study,

[1]Justin Pope, "Books Examine Jesus, as Part of U.S. History, Culture," *Chicago Sun-Times,* February 13, 2004, 48.

we will evaluate what they had to say and how it still impacts us today.

Join me on this journey as we explore the origins of the Christian faith.

Dr. Erwin W. Lutzer

PREFACE
THE DA VINCI CODE AT A GLANCE

Welcome to the mysterious world of conspiracy, secret codes, and historical documents hidden for as many centuries as the church has existed!

If you've not read *The Da Vinci Code,* I'll introduce you to the story and to some novel ideas you might not have heard before, such as:

- Jesus was married to Mary Magdalene!
- They had children who intermarried with the French royal line!
- And all this has been known for centuries, but the truth has been kept from the public for fear of destroying the power of the church! In fact, there

is a highly secret organization that guards documents that, if made public, would destroy Christianity as we know it!

"Rumors of this conspiracy have been whispered for centuries," says best-selling author Dan Brown in *The Da Vinci Code*. In fact, these rumors have appeared "in countless languages, including the languages of art, music, and literature." And, we are told, some of the most dramatic evidence appears in the paintings of Leonardo da Vinci.

The Da Vinci Code has been on the best-seller lists for months, and with a 2006 movie based on the book, the story is receiving even wider circulation. If you've not read the novel, you probably know someone who has. Many are thinking that the book just might have some plausibility. Perhaps the historical evidence is shaky, but, as one reviewer asked, "Why can't we believe that it *might* have happened?"

Before we answer that question, let's take a look at the book's premise. In brief, here's the story: *The Da Vinci Code* opens with the curator of the Louvre lying dead in a pool of his own blood. Meanwhile, Robert Langdon, a Harvard professor and expert in esoteric symbolism, is in Paris on business. The French police track Langdon down at his hotel and ask him to interpret a strange cipher left on the body of the murder victim. Langdon is joined in his investigation by a young cryptologist named Sophie Neveu.

When Sophie privately warns Robert that he is the prime suspect in the murder, they flee. But the murder victim has intentionally left clues for them to follow. As they decipher his coded instructions, Robert and Sophie quickly realize that the crime is linked to the legendary search for the Holy Grail. Quite providentially, the pair is able to link up with a Holy Grail fanatic, Sir Leigh Teabing, whose extensive knowledge and research fuel their efforts to find the Grail.

Teabing enthusiastically instructs the pair on matters that surround the events of the New Testament, including an alternate understanding of Jesus, Mary Magdalene, and the true nature of the Holy Grail. He cites the Gnostic Gospels, ancient documents that supposedly give a more reliable account of Christ's life and teachings than the New Testament documents we know today.

Still sought by the authorities, Robert, Sophie,

and now Sir Leigh flee to London and later Scotland, hoping to find more evidence about the murder and its connection to the Holy Grail. The reader is kept in suspense as these smart and determined characters pierce the hidden world of mystery and conspiracy in an attempt to overcome centuries of deceit and secrecy. Staying one step ahead of the police, they are able to use hidden codes and manuscripts that the church has tried to hide from the public.

Perhaps the most interesting part of the book—and lying at the heart of it—is the notion that Jesus was married to Mary Magdalene and they had a daughter. Legend has it that after Jesus' crucifixion, Mary and her daughter, Sarah, went to Gaul, where they established the Merovingian line of French royalty. This dynasty, we are told, continues even today in the mysterious organization known as the Priory of Sion, a secret organization whose military wing was the Knights Templar. Members of this organization supposedly include Leonardo da Vinci, Isaac Newton, and Victor Hugo. To this day, says Teabing, the relics of Mary and the records excavated by the Templars are guarded, shrouded in secrecy and mystery.

There is more: *The Da Vinci Code* reinterprets the Holy Grail as none other than the remains of Jesus' wife, Mary Magdalene, who held the blood of Jesus Christ in her womb while bearing his child.

The book claims that Jesus intended Mary Magdalene to lead the church, but "Peter had a problem with that," thus she was declared a prostitute and cut out of the role of leadership. Apparently, the church wanted a celibate male savior who would perpetuate male rule. So, after her husband was crucified, Mary disappeared with her child, resurfacing in Gaul. If this theory were true, descendents of Jesus could still be alive today.

Robert and Sir Leigh tell Sophie that the real story about Mary has been preserved in carefully hidden codes and symbols in order to avert the wrath of the Catholic Church. In these hidden codes, the Priory of Sion has been able to preserve its own version of Jesus and Mary's life together without telling the whole truth.

Leonardo da Vinci knew all this, we are told, and used his well-known painting *The Last Supper* to conceal many levels of meaning. In the painting John is sitting to the right of Jesus. But John's features are feminine; it turns out that the person to the right of Jesus is not John after all, but rather Mary Magdalene. And, tellingly, Leonardo did not paint a cup or chalice on the table—another hint that the real Grail is Mary, sitting to the right of Jesus!

While Robert, Sophie, and Sir Leigh continue their investigation, the powerful Catholic organization Opus Dei is ready to use whatever means necessary—including assassination—to keep a lid on the secret. Flush with church money, Opus Dei is determined to force the top officials of the Priory to reveal the map to the Grail's location. If the secrets of the Priory were revealed, the church

IS *THE DA VINCI CODE* TRUE?

The first pages acknowledge that the story is fiction, but that the facts within it (dates, documents, historical figures, etc.) are true. This has led to great confusion for many readers about how to distinguish what is fact and what is myth. Also, because Dan Brown quotes historical sources, the novel gives the illusion of being factual even in those matters where it can be shown to be fraudulent. Hopefully, the book you are now reading will clarify where the history ends and the fiction begins.

would be exposed as a fraud built on centuries of deceit.

Dan Brown's agenda is not so thinly veiled: This book is a direct attack against Jesus Christ, the church, and those of us who are his followers and call him Savior and Lord. Christianity, according to Dan Brown's novel, was invented to suppress women and to turn people away from the "divine feminine." Understandably, the book appeals to feminists, who see a return to goddess worship as a necessity to combat male supremacy.

The upshot of this theory is that Christianity is based on a big lie, or rather, several big lies. For one thing, Jesus was not God, but his followers attributed deity to him in order to consolidate male rule and to suppress those who worshipped the divine feminine. Indeed, according to Dan Brown, at the Council of Nicaea Constantine invented the idea of the deity of Christ so that he could eliminate all opposition, declaring those who disagreed to be heretics. Further, Constantine also chose Matthew, Mark, Luke, and John as the only Gospels because they fit his agenda of male power. Eighty other viable Gospels were rejected because they taught that Jesus wanted Mary Magdalene to be the real leader of the church. "It was all about power," we're told.

Incredibly, we learn that in the Old Testament, Israel worshipped both the male God Jehovah and his *feminine counterpart*, the Shekinah. Centuries later, the official church—the sex-hating, woman-hating church—suppressed this goddess worship and eliminated the divine feminine.

This concept of the divine feminine, which the church tried to suppress, is actually the pagan notion that in sex rituals the male and female experience God. "Physical union with the female remained the sole means through which man could become spiritually complete and ultimately achieve *gnosis*—knowledge of the divine."[1] But this use of sex to commune directly with God posed a threat to the Catholic Church because it undermined its power. "For obvious reasons, they worked hard to demonize sex and recast it as a disgusting and sinful act. Other major religions did the same."[2]

"Almost everything our fathers taught us about Christ is *false*," laments Teabing. The New Testament is simply the result of a male-dominated leadership that invented Christianity in order to control the Roman Empire and to oppress women. The real Jesus was the original feminist, but his wishes were ignored to foster the male agenda.

If *The DaVinci Code* were billed as just a novel, it would be an interesting read for conspiracy buffs who like a fast-paced thriller. What makes the book troublesome is that it purports to be based on facts. In the flyleaf, we read that the Priory of Sion exists, as does Opus Dei, a deeply devout Catholic sect that is controversial due to reports of brainwashing, coercion, and "corporal mortification." Finally, we are told, "All descriptions of artwork, architecture, documents, and secret rituals in this novel are accurate."

On his Web site, Dan Brown makes other statements about the historical reliability of the work. Some reviewers have praised the book for its "impeccable research." One woman, when told that the novel was bunk, replied, "If it were not true it could not have been published!" One man said now that he has read the book, he will never be able to enter a church again.

Readers should know that the basic plot of this book has existed for centuries and can be found in esoteric and New Age literature such as *Holy Blood,*

Holy Grail by Michael Baigent (1983), which is referenced in the novel. The difference is that Brown takes these legends and wraps them in a quasi-historical story that is being read by millions. Many who read the book are wondering if all, or at least some, of its claims might be true.

When ABC did a documentary on *The Da Vinci Code*, it gave credence to the novel and, for the most part, ignored serious scholarship in favor of sensationalist rumor and ill-founded speculation. Although the program ended with the statement, "We don't have any proof," it's clear that the book was given some degree of respectability, with the implication that proof or not, Dan Brown just might be onto something.

Recently I read *The Templar Revelation: Secret Guardians of the True Identity of Christ*, written by Lynn Pickett and Clive Prince, which includes similar themes to *The Da Vinci Code* supposedly based on historical research. This book attempts to give validity to the idea that Mary Magdalene was the woman Jesus appointed to begin the church. It also contends that the New Testament is a sanitized account of cultic themes, including sex rituals.

How plausible is it that a conspiracy has kept

the real story of Mary and Jesus under wraps? If it is true, the entire structure of Christian theology is a plot to deceive the masses. If it is true, the apostles were all party to this plot and were willing to give their lives for what they knew to be a lie. And if it is true, our faith—the faith of those of us who trust in Christ—is groundless.

UNCOVERING THE DECEPTION

Since *The Da Vinci Code* claims to be quasi-historical, it is important for us to ask: Is this book plausible? Many are wondering where Brown crosses the line between truth and fiction, between fact and fantasy. Is it just possible that someday, somewhere, we will discover that his version of history has credibility?

I've written this book in an attempt to answer these and other questions. We'll look at topics such as the Council of Nicaea, the Gnostic Gospels, the canon of the New Testament, and the paintings of Leonardo da Vinci. Was Jesus simply an inspiring leader who founded a religious movement? Did the Gnostics represent an early form of Christianity that was hijacked by the male-dominated apostles of the New Testament? In the process of answering these questions, I trust that your faith will be both challenged and strengthened.

It is not my intention to list all of the historical errors in *The Da Vinci Code*—that would be a lengthy list indeed. These false statements included: "Jesus was a historical figure of staggering influence . . . (he) inspired millions" when he was here on earth and "during three hundred years of witch hunts, the Church burned at the stake an astounding five *million* women."[3] These and other misstatements aren't really central to the basic attack the book makes against the Christian faith. I plan to focus instead on the scurrilous remarks made against Jesus and the Bible.

Following are several of the key questions we'll attempt to answer:

- Did Constantine invent the deity of Christ? And did the Council of Nicaea, which he convened, determine which books should be in the New Testament?
- Are the Gnostic Gospels reliable guides to New Testament history?
- Who determined what books would constitute the New Testament, and on what basis were the

books included? When were these decisions made?

- Is it plausible that Mary Magdalene was married to Jesus?
- Was Opus Dei charged with destroying the Priory of Sion in order to suppress secrets about the real Jesus?
- Is it true that Gnosticism (to be defined later) is a viable "alternative Christianity" that might represent the true Christian faith?
- If we agree on God, do we also have to agree about Jesus?

Come with me on a journey that will lead us into the intriguing story of the origins of Christianity and those historical events that defined the Christian church.

Whether or not you have read *The Da Vinci Code*, I think you'll benefit from a Christian response to the attacks being made against the Jesus of history.

ONE
CHRISTIANITY, A POLITICIAN, AND A CREED

We have good reason to be skeptical when a politician embraces religion—especially if religion helps him achieve his political ambitions.

Consider the emperor Constantine, who in *The Da Vinci Code* is said to have invented the deity of Christ in order to consolidate his power. And, we're told, he also eliminated those books from the New Testament that did not suit his political agenda.

In *The Da Vinci Code*, Brown asserts that by declaring the deity of Christ, Constantine solidified his rule and earned the right to declare those who disagreed with him as heretics. The emperor convened the Council of Nicaea in AD 325 to ratify this new doctrine that would give him the clout he craved. Sir Leigh Teabing, the Holy Grail enthusiast, explains to Sophie that at the council the delegates agreed on the divinity of Jesus. Then he adds, "Until *that* moment in history, Jesus was viewed by His followers as a mortal prophet . . . a great and powerful man, but a *man* nonetheless. A mortal."

So Constantine "upgraded Jesus' status almost three centuries *after* Jesus' death" for political reasons.[1] In the process, he secured male dominance and the suppression of women. By forcing others to accept his views, the emperor demonstrated his power and was free to kill all who opposed him.

The second allegation in the novel is that Constantine rejected other gospels that were favorable to the divine feminine. To quote Teabing again, "More than *eighty* gospels were considered for the New Testament, and yet only a relative few were chosen for inclusion—Matthew, Mark, Luke, and John among them . . . . The Bible, as we know it today, was collated by the pagan Roman emperor Constantine the Great."[2]

In other words, Constantine recognized a good deal when he saw it and therefore called the council to ensure male power and accept those canonical documents that were favorable to his political agenda. In the novel, Langdon says, "The Priory believes that Constantine and his male successors successfully converted the world from matriarchal paganism to patriarchal Christianity by waging a campaign of propaganda that demonized the sacred feminine, obliterating the goddess from modern religion forever."[3] With this accomplishment, the course of church history was solidified according to Constantine's liking. "Remember it was all about power," we are told.

Let's begin to investigate these claims. In this chapter we'll separate fact from fiction, look into the ancient records, and discover exactly what Constantine did and didn't do.

Church historians agree that next to the events in the New Testament, the most important event in the history of Christianity is the conversion of Emperor Constantine to Christianity in AD 312. In brief, here's the story: Constantine's troops were positioned at the Milvian Bridge just outside of Rome, where they were preparing to overthrow the Roman emperor Maxentius. A victory would, in effect, make Constantine the sole ruler of the empire. But the night before the battle, Constantine saw a vision that changed his life and the history of the church.

In the words of Eusebius of Caesarea, who was both a historian and a confidant of Constantine, the emperor was praying to a pagan god when "he saw with his own eyes the trophy of a cross in the light of the heavens, above the sun and an inscription, *Conquer By This* attached to it. . . . Then in his sleep the Christ of God appeared to him with the sign which he had seen in the heavens, and commanded him to make a likeness of this sign which he had seen in the heavens, and to use it as a safeguard in all engagements with his enemies."[4]

To make a long story short, Constantine crossed over the bridge and won the battle, fighting under the banner of the Christian cross. Later he issued the Edict of Milan, decreeing that Christians were no longer to be persecuted. And now, although a politician, he took leadership in the doctrinal disputes that were disrupting the unity in his empire.

Let's travel back to Nicaea (modern-day Iznik in Turkey, about 125 miles from modern-day Istanbul) to find out what happened there 1,700 years ago.

WELCOME TO THE COUNCIL

Those of us reared in a country where religion is largely private and where diversity is gladly tolerated might find it difficult to believe that in the early fourth century, doctrinal disputes were tearing Constantine's empire apart. It is said that if you bought a loaf of bread in the marketplace of Constantinople, you might be asked whether you believe that God the Son was begotten or unbegotten and if you asked about the quality of the bread you might be told that the Father is greater and the Son is less.

Adding fuel to these disagreements was a man named Arius, who was gaining a wide following by teaching that Christ was not fully God but a created god of sorts. He believed that Christ was more than a man but less than God. Arius was a great communicator, and because he put his doctrinal ideas into musical jingles, his ideas became widely accepted. Although many church bishops declared him a heretic, the disputes nonetheless continued. Constantine called the first ecumenical council at Nicaea, hoping to suppress dissent and unify Christianity. In fact, the emperor even paid the expenses of the bishops who gathered.

Constantine did not care about the finer points of theology, so practically any creed would have satisfied him—as long as it would unify his subjects. As one historian has said, "Christianity became both a way to God and a way to unite the empire."[5] He gave the opening speech himself, telling the delegates that doctrinal disunity was worse than war.

This intrusion of a politician into the doctrines and procedures of the church was resented by some of the delegates, but welcomed by others. For those who had gone through a period of bitter persecution, this conference, carried on under the imperial banner, was heaven on earth.

THE GREAT DEBATE

More than three hundred bishops met at Nicaea to settle disputes about Christology—that is, the doctrine of Christ. When Constantine finished his opening speech, the proceedings began.

Overwhelmingly, the council declared Arius a heretic. Though Arius was given an opportunity to defend his views, the delegates recognized that if Christ was not fully God, then God was not the Redeemer of mankind. To say that Christ was created was to deny the clear teaching of Scripture: "For by him all things were created: things in heaven and on earth, visible and invisible, whether thrones or powers or rulers or authorities; all things were created by him and for him" (Colossians 1:16). Clearly, if he created *all* things, he most assuredly could not have been created himself! To this passage many others that teach the deity of Christ were added, both from the Gospels and the Epistles (John 1:1; Romans 9:5; Hebrews 1:8; etc.).

Affirming the divinity of Jesus, the delegates turned their attention to the question of how he related to the Father. Eusebius the historian presented his view, claiming that Jesus had a nature that was *similar* to that of God the Father.

Present, but not invited to the actual proceedings, was the theologian Athanasius, who believed that even to say that Christ is *similar* to God the Father is to miss the full biblical teaching about Christ's divinity. His argument that Christ could only be God in the fullest sense if his nature was the *same* as that of the Father was expressed by his representative, Marcellus, a bishop from Asia Minor in the proceedings. Constantine, seeing that the debate was going in Athanasius's favor, accepted the suggestion of a scholarly bishop and advised the delegates to use the Greek word *homoousion*, which means "one and the same." In other words, Jesus had the very *same* nature as the Father.

The council agreed, and today we have the famous Nicene Creed. As anyone who has ever quoted the creed knows, Jesus Christ is declared to be "Light of Light, very God of very God; begotten, not made, *being of one substance* with the Father, by whom all things were made" (italics added). There can be no question that the delegates affirmed that Christ was deity in the fullest sense.

Why should we be interested in this debate? Some critics have been amused that the Council of Nicaea split over one "iota." The difference between the Greek words for *similar* and *same* is but one letter of the alphabet: the letter *i*. Some argue that it's just like theologians to split hairs, arguing over minutiae that have little to do with the real world. How much better to help the poor or get involved in the politics of the day!

But William E. Hordern tells a story that illustrates how a single letter or comma can change the meaning of a message. Back in the days when messages were sent by telegraph there was a code for each punctuation mark. A woman touring Europe cabled her husband to ask whether she could buy a beautiful bracelet for $75,000. The husband sent this message back: "No, price too high." The cable operator, in transmitting the message, missed the signal for the comma. The woman received the message "No price too high." She bought the bracelet; the husband sued the company and won! After that, people using Morse code spelled out all punctuation. Clearly, a comma or an "iota" can make a big difference when communicating a message![6]

Although the Council of Nicaea was divided over the Greek words *similar* and *same,* the issue was incredibly important. Even if Christ were the highest and most noble creature of God's creation, God would then be only indirectly involved in the salvation of man. As one historian has said, Athanasius realized that "only if Christ is God, without qualification, has God entered humanity, and only then have fellowship with God, the forgiveness of sins, the truth of God, and immortality been certainly brought to men."[7]

In *The Da Vinci Code,* we read that the doctrine of Christ's deity passed by a "relatively close vote."

That is fiction, since only five out of more than three hundred bishops (the number is actually believed to have been 318) protested the creed. In fact, in the end, only two refused to sign it. The outcome was not exactly a cliff-hanger.

That's not to say that the Council of Nicaea ended all the disputes. Arianism continued to have its adherents, and subsequent emperors sided with whichever view suited them at the time. But from this point on, Christian orthodoxy maintained that Jesus was "God of very God."

Whether Constantine was a genuine convert to Christianity is a matter of debate. We do know that he had been a worshipper of the sun god before his "conversion," and it appears that he carried on such worship for the rest of his life. He is even credited with standardizing Christian worship by mandating Sunday as the official day of worship. There is no doubt that he used Christianity to further his own political ends.

But did he invent the divinity of Jesus? Before the council, was Christ believed to be just a remarkable man? There is not a single shred of historical evidence for such a notion. Not only was Christ's deity the consensus of the delegates, but

DID EMPEROR CONSTANTINE REINVENT CHRISTIANITY FOR HIS OWN PURPOSES?

Doctrinal disputes were tearing Constantine's empire apart, so at the urging of bishops, he called the Council of Nicaea that affirmed that Christ was "God of very God." Constantine cared little about the finer points of theology, so practically any creed would have satisfied him—as long as it would unify his subjects. But did he invent the divinity of Jesus? There is not a shred of historical evidence for such a notion. As can easily be shown in the writings of early church fathers, this doctrine was held by the church centuries *before* the council of Nicaea met in 325.

as can easily be shown, this doctrine was held by the church centuries *before* the council met.

Contrary to Teabing's claim in *The Da Vinci Code,* many believed that Christ was more than a "mortal prophet" before the council met in AD 325. We must take a moment to read the writings of the apostolic fathers, those who knew the apostles and were taught by them. Then we can investigate writings of the second- and third-generation leaders, all affirming in their own way the divinity of Jesus.

THE CHURCH FATHERS

Let me introduce you to someone who longed to die for Jesus. That was the attitude of Ignatius, the bishop of Antioch in Syria. In AD 110, he wrote a series of letters to several churches while on his way to martyrdom in Rome. The centerpiece of his doctrine was his conviction that Christ is God Incarnate. "There is One God who manifests himself through Jesus Christ his son."[8] Another source elaborates further: Ignatius speaks of Jesus as "Son of Mary and Son of God . . . Jesus Christ our Lord," calling Jesus "God Incarnate." In fact, he refers to him as "Christ God."[9] Remember, he wrote this a full two hundred years *before* the Council of Nicaea!

Other examples include the following:

- Polycarp of Smyrna, a disciple of the apostle John, sent a letter to the church at Philippi in about AD 112–118. In it, he assumes that those to whom it is addressed acknowledge the divinity of Jesus, his exaltation to heaven, and his subsequent glorification. Polycarp was martyred in about AD 160 and gave testimony of his faith in the presence of his executioners.[10]

- Justin Martyr was born in Palestine and was impressed with the ability of Christians to face death heroically. When he heard the gospel, he converted to Christianity and became a defender of the faith he loved. He said Christ was "the son and the apostle of God the Father and master of all."[11] He was born about AD 100 and martyred in AD 165.
- Irenaeus became the bishop of Lyons in AD 177. He spent much of his life combating the heresy of Gnosticism that we will examine in the next chapter. Speaking of passages such as John 1:1, he wrote that "all distinctions between the Father and the Son vanish, for the one God made all things through His word."[12]

To this list could be added teachers like Tertullian (150–212), who one hundred years before Constantine advocated a fully divine and fully human Christ. Dozens of other writings from the early centuries of Christianity prove that the early church affirmed the deity of Jesus. Their convictions were rooted in the New Testament Scriptures that were already accepted as authoritative by the church. For the two and a half centuries *before* Nicaea, the nearly universal opinion of the church was that Christ was divine, just as the Scriptures taught.

THE WITNESS OF THE MARTYRS

We find more evidence that the divinity of Christ was not Constantine's idea when we remind ourselves of the persecutions in Rome. If we had belonged to a small congregation in Rome in the second or third century, we might have heard an announcement like this: "The emperor [Caesar Augustus] has issued a new order, requiring all Roman subjects to attend the religious/political ceremony designed to unify the nation and revive lagging patriotism within the empire." The Romans believed that if one had a god above Caesar, that person could not be trusted at a time of national emergency—a war, for instance. All good citizens were commanded to "worship the spirit of Rome and the genius of the emperor," as the edict read. Specifically, this ceremony involved the burning of incense and saying simply, "Caesar is Lord."

Sometimes persecution was directly targeted against those who worshipped Jesus. But for the most part, Caesar did not care what god a person worshipped. After one made the yearly obligatory confession that Caesar was Lord, that person was free to worship whatever god he or she wished—including Jesus. Christian congregations—and there were many of them—had to make a tough choice: They either complied as citizens or faced cruel retribution. Many of the Christians had watched as their relatives and friends were thrown to wild beasts or killed by gladiators for refusing to confess Caesar's lordship.

If Jesus were seen as one option among many, Christians could give allegiance to other expressions of the divine. Why not find common ground with the central unity of all religions? Not only would this have promoted harmony, but also the common good of the state. So the choice, strictly speaking, was not whether the Christians would worship Christ or Caesar but whether they would worship Christ *and* Caesar.

If you ever have the opportunity to visit Rome, don't miss the Pantheon, one of the most ancient and beautiful buildings still standing today, completed in AD 126. It is a masterpiece of perfection with a grand hemispherical dome. This was the Roman "temple of the gods," the place where all the various gods of ancient Rome were housed.

Filled with statues and artifacts, it is here that Rome's diverse religious worship was localized.

Interestingly, the pagans saw no conflict between emperor worship and the worship of their own gods. Paganism, both ancient and modern, has always been tolerant of other finite gods. After all, if your god is not a supreme deity, then indeed you have little choice but to make room for other gods and celebrate the splendor of diversity.

But the Christians understood something very clearly: If Christ was God—and they believed he was—indeed, if he was "God of very God," then they could not worship him and others. Thus, while some bowed to Caesar in order to save their life and their family, many of them—thousands of them—were willing to defy the political authorities and pay dearly for their commitment.

After an intense time of persecution for those who affirmed the divinity of Jesus, the unexpected happened. The emperor decided that the persecution of Christians should end. To make good on his word, he commissioned that a statue of Jesus be put in the Pantheon as an expression of goodwill and proof that Jesus was now regarded as a legitimate god, along with all the rest. But the Christians said,

HOW CLOSE WAS THE VOTE WHEN THE COUNCIL OF NICAEA DEVELOPED THEIR CREED ABOUT JESUS' DIVINITY?

In *The Da Vinci Code*, we read that the doctrine of Christ's deity passed by a "relatively close vote." That is fiction, since only five out of more than three hundred bishops protested the creed. In the end, only two refused to sign it. The outcome was not exactly a cliff-hanger.

in effect, "Thanks, but no thanks." They understood that the divinity of Jesus meant that he could not be put on the same shelf as the pagan gods.

My point is simply that centuries before Constantine, these early Christians had already proved that they believed that Jesus was divine. And they paid for their convictions with reprisals, harassment, and often death. *The Da Vinci Code*'s assertion that Constantine "upgraded Jesus' status" from man to God is pure fiction.

No wonder the mark of a heretic in New Testament times was someone who denied the Incarnation. "Every spirit that acknowledges that Jesus Christ has come in the flesh is from God, but every spirit that does not acknowledge Jesus is not from God" (1 John 4:2-3). The conviction that, in

Christ, God became man was the heart of the early Christian faith.

THE COUNCIL OF NICAEA AND THE NEW TESTAMENT CANON

The Da Vinci Code claims—as do many occult writings—that Constantine and his delegates decided to eliminate books from the New Testament that were unfavorable to their theology of male rule and their commitment to sexual repression. We've already quoted Sir Leigh Teabing as saying that more than eighty gospels were considered for the New Testament and that the Bible as we know it today was collated by Constantine.

I read a similar view in *The Templar Revelation*, a book that dovetails with *The Da Vinci Code,* supposedly giving historical plausibility to these events. The authors allege: "In our opinion, the Catholic Church never wanted its members to know about the true relationship between Jesus and Mary, which is why the Gnostic Gospels were not included in the New Testament and why most Christians do not even know they exist. The Council of Nicaea, when it rejected the many Gnostic Gospels and voted to include only Matthew,

Mark, Luke and John in the New Testament, had no divine mandate for this major act of censorship. They acted out of self-preservation, for by that time—the fourth century—the power of the Magdalene and her followers was already too widespread for the patriarchy to cope with."[13]

We'll look closer at matters regarding the formation of the canon and the life of Mary Magdalene later in this book. But for now, consider this: Historical works on Nicaea give no evidence that Constantine and the delegates even discussed the Gnostic Gospels or anything that pertained to the canon. Try as I might, I have not found a single line in the documents about Nicaea that records a discussion about what books should or should not be in the New Testament. Practically everything we know about what happened at Nicaea comes from the historian Eusebius, and neither he nor anyone else gives a hint that such matters were discussed. Twenty rulings were issued at Nicaea, and the contents of all of them are still in existence; not one of them refers to issues regarding the canon.

Thankfully, I was able to track down the source of the error. Baron D'Holbach in *Ecce Homo* writes, "The question of authentic and spurious gospels was not discussed at the first Nicene Council. The anecdote is fictitious."[14] D'Holbach traces the fiction to Voltaire, but further research reveals an even earlier source of the rumor.

An anonymous document called *Vetus Synodicon*, written in about AD 887, devotes a chapter to each of the ecumenical councils held until that time. However, the compiler adds details not found in the writings of historians. As for his account of Nicaea, he writes that the council dealt with matters of the divinity of Jesus, the Trinity, and the canon. He writes, "The canonical and apocryphal books it distinguished in the following manner: in the house of God the books were placed down by the holy altar; then the council asked the Lord in prayer that the inspired works be found on top and—as in fact happened. . . ."[15] That, quite obviously, is the stuff of legend. No primary documents pertaining to Nicaea make reference to such a procedure.

Even if this story were true, it would still not prove the claim that the council rejected certain books of the New Testament because they promoted feminism or the notion that Mary Magdalene was married to Jesus. These matters simply did not come up for discussion.

DID THE COUNCIL OF NICAEA INVENT OR CREATE THE MODERN NEW TESTAMENT?

Historical works on Nicaea give no evidence that Constantine and the delegates discussed what books should be in the canon. Twenty rulings were issued at Nicaea; not one of them refers to issues regarding which books were authoritative.

Legends developed in the ninth century attached all kinds of fictitious stories to the historical accounts of the church councils. Among them was the notion that Constantine and the delegates censored the documents and chose those they wanted for their own purposes. No primary documents pertaining to Nicaea support this idea.

Speaking of legends, another claims that after the two bishops who did not sign the Nicene Creed died, the church fathers, not willing to alter the miraculous number of 318 (apparently the number of delegates present), placed the creed sans their signature in their tombs overnight, "whereupon miraculously their signatures were also added."[16] These kinds of superstitions flourished through medieval times.

Later, we'll learn that Constantine did ask that

fifty Bibles be copied for the churches of Constantinople. But *The Da Vinci Code*'s assertion that Constantine tampered with the Scriptures or excluded certain books is bogus. This is a reminder that legends are often confused with facts in such a way that the legends appear to replace the facts. When one presents history without consulting the sources, anything the mind can imagine can be written. As fabrications go, *The Da Vinci Code* is right up there with Elvis sightings.

HISTORY REPEATS ITSELF

We've learned that the official Roman government abhorred the exclusivism of Christianity, the idea that Christ is the only way to God. The Romans bristled at the very suggestion that Christ stood above other gods—indeed, claiming that no other gods even existed. To them, it was both politically and religiously intolerable for Christians to insist that there was only one legitimate Redeemer who was willing to come to the aid of mankind. They were tolerant of everyone except those who were intolerant.

In the next chapter we will see that another powerful attack against the Christian faith came

not from the political establishment but from religious zealots who wanted to make Christianity
doctrinally diverse. Although Gnosticism was a religious and not a political movement, it had the
same motivation as the Roman government—it
could not tolerate the exclusive claims made by
Jesus Christ. Gnostics cynically used the Christian
faith as it suited them rather than accepting what
they regarded as the narrow doctrines taught by
the early church.

As we investigate Gnosticism, we will see that it
bears striking similarities to the modern-day
quest for spirituality. Gnosticism invites its followers to divide loyalties between Jesus and lesser
competing deities. Gnosticism says our real need
is not for forgiveness but for self-enlightenment.
Jesus, claim the Gnostics, can help us, but he is not
necessary to our quest for salvation.

Gnosticism rejects the conclusion of Nicaea,
unless of course, we are all seen as divine. Like the
New Agers of today, Gnostics believed that each
person can encounter God in his own way. Little
wonder Paul wrote, "For the time will come when
men will not put up with sound doctrine. Instead,
to suit their own desires, they will gather around

them a great number of teachers to say what their itching ears want to hear" (2 Timothy 4:3).

Join me as we investigate the Gnostic documents.

TWO

THAT OTHER BIBLE

Did you know there is another Bible for sale in your local bookstore? I'm not referring to a new translation of the Bible, but an entirely different one—a Bible with about fifty books. Some of these books have names like *The Gospel of Thomas, The Gospel of Philip, The Gospel of Mary,* and *The Gospel of Truth*.

Welcome to *The Gnostic Bible,* which I have open before me as I write this chapter. Some people like this alternate Bible better than the one we're ac-quainted with; they like what it teaches about God, Christ, mankind, and women. This Bible gives us permission to make God into whoever we want him (or her) to be. This Bible accepts the divine feminine and personal esoteric knowledge. At last we are free from restricting doctrines such as the Virgin Birth, the unique deity of Christ, and his resurrection. This new Bible is broad enough to embrace our culture and lets us believe pretty much whatever we wish to believe.

There is a growing perception that an alternate canon has been discovered that gives us a different way of "being Christian." The argument is that these so-called Gnostic Gospels give us a more reliable account of the life of Jesus and his teachings than the canonical Gospels. The Gnostic Gospels, some would say, are a better representation of early Christianity than the Bible that most of us grew up with.

The introduction of *The Gnostic Bible* says, "We are presenting these texts as sacred books and sacred scriptures of the Gnostics and, collectively, as sacred literature of the Gnostics."[1] So, side by side with our standard Bible, we now have competing "sacred" texts.

In *The Da Vinci Code*, the Gnostic Gospels provide the historical basis for the alleged marriage of Jesus to Mary Magdalene, supposedly referred to in *The Gospel of Philip*. In the novel, Sir Leigh Teabing quotes the passage and says, "Unfortunately for the early editors, one particularly troubling earthly theme kept recurring in the gospels. Mary Magdalene. . . . More specifically, her marriage to Jesus Christ."[2] Later in the novel, *The Gospel of Mary* is quoted to show that it was Jesus' intention for Mary Magdalene to become the leader of the church.

Since the supposed marriage of Jesus and Mary Magdalene lies at the heart of *The Da Vinci Code*, we'll look more closely at that question in the next chapter. Here I simply want to give a brief introduction to the Gnostic Gospels so we can better understand their origin and teachings.

The word *Gnostic* comes from the Greek *gnosis*, which means "knowledge." More precisely, the word is used to refer to hidden knowledge that is available only to the enlightened. The Gnostics believed they were privy to spiritual experiences that gave them an inside track on a religious interpretation of the world. Their version of Christianity was, among other things, profeminine. God is sometimes described as androgynous—that is, both male and female. Some of these writings speak of sexual rituals, and others make convoluted references to teachings about Jesus and his disciples. Understandably, these writings are used in feminist literature in an attempt to redefine Christianity and disclose the "real story" regarding the origins of Christianity.

"Dozens of Christian Scriptures were Holy Writ, then heresy, then forgotten. Why are we looking at them again?"[3] These were the questions *Time* magazine asked in its cover story on these gospels. We are told these gospels "fill a perceived need for alternative views of the Christ story on the part of New Age seekers and of mainline believers uncomfortable with some of their faith's theological restrictions."[4] Some church study groups, the article says, are reading these alternative gospels and are finding them to be in harmony with the present spirit of tolerance and do-it-yourself religion.

Since the Bible—the traditional one—has stood the test of time and the disciplines of history and archaeology, is it not only fair that we critique *The Gnostic Bible* with the same historical scrutiny that the more familiar Bible has received? Unfortunately, this is both more difficult and easier at the

WHAT ABOUT THE SECRET GOSPELS THAT GIVE US OTHER DETAILS ABOUT JESUS' LIFE?

There is a collection of books called the Secret Gospels that give far-fetched details about the early life of Jesus. The leaders of the church recognized these to be tales hatched in fertile imaginations. History shows that legends always develop around famous figures, and we should not be surprised that some people would attach superstitions to Jesus. These books were never seriously considered as part of canonical Scripture.

same time. More difficult, because *The Gnostic Bible* makes no references to cities, rivers, valleys, and specific sequential events as does our traditional Bible. For the most part the Gnostic Gospels make no pretense of being an actual record of events; rather, they are simply the musings of various teachers. In fact, as we'll see later, the Gnostic writers did not actually believe that historical events (such as the life and mission of Jesus) were essential to the spiritual quest.

On the other hand, it is easier to critique these gospels because we know enough about the Gnostics and their *modus operandi* to call their reliability into question. To put it mildly, there is no reason to accept the Gnostic Gospels as historically worthy; their value lies in telling us what the Gnostics believed, even though the writings shed no new light on Jesus, Mary Magdalene, or early Christianity.

However, since these gospels are frequently quoted in *The Da Vinci Code* and are widely used in various occult interpretations of the New Testament, we must take a close look at their origin and content. We're engaged in nothing less than the battle for the real Bible.

FINDING THE GNOSTIC WRITINGS

In 1945 an Arab peasant in Egypt digging for fertilizer uncovered a red earthenware jar. He had hoped to find gold, but as someone once said, what he actually found was something more precious than gold. Inside the jar were thirteen leather-bound papyrus books written in Coptic. Although some of the manuscripts were burned or disfigured, a number were intact. Obviously, no one knows when these were buried, but the dates of the actual writing of the originals range from about AD 150 to the fourth or fifth century. Scholars translated these documents into English so we can read them for ourselves. These writings, along with other selections from Jewish and even Chinese sources, are all found in *The Gnostic Bible*.

Some brief background is in order: The Gnostics were a group of thinkers who were highly influenced by Plato. They differed among themselves about many issues, making it difficult to summarize in a few sentences what exactly they believed. Suffice it to say that most of them denied the idea of God becoming flesh, because matter was regarded as evil and hence God could not have become man. They speculated about the origin of evil and its relationship to creation. Man must find his own way to salvation, they claimed, and his problem is not *sin* but rather *the need for self-knowledge*.

Some Gnostics clearly accepted a deity that was both feminine and masculine. They almost universally denied the physical resurrection of Jesus; some even taught that Jesus did not die on the cross, but that a substitute died for him. Though they differed regarding how salvation was attained, they did agree that redemption is within our power, and that it can be achieved by encountering the divine directly without the mediation of Christ or the church.

As we might expect, the teachings of the Gnostics have been known and studied from earliest times. In fact, Irenaeus, in the second century wrote the book *Against Heresies,* in which he expounded the teachings of the Gnostics and why Christians regarded them as heretics. So in a sense, these present documents provide very little that is new. What is new is the popular fascination with these writings because of the religious climate in the United States. To quote Marcus Borg, author of *The Heart of Christianity,* "There is a lot of interest in early Christian diversity because many people who have left the church—and some who are still in it—are looking for another way of being Christian."[5]

AN EVALUATION OF THE GNOSTIC BIBLE

Come with me on a tour of *The Gnostic Bible.* As we've learned, some of the writings have names that are familiar to us: *The Gospel of Peter, The Gospel of Mary, The Gospel of Philip,* and *The Gospel of Thomas.* So whatever these "gospels" are, there is no doubt that the authors tried to give the distinct impression that they are based on Christian sources.

But how credible are they?

SPURIOUS AUTHORSHIP

To begin with, not even the most radical liberal scholar seriously believes that *The Gospel of Thomas* was written by the Thomas of the New Testament or that *The Gospel of Philip* was written by the Philip of the New Testament. The same can be said for other Gnostic Gospels that bear the names of the early apostles. As we shall see, the dates of the documents and the locations in which they were written demonstrate that they were simply attributed to apostles to give them credibility and the impression that they are an early version of Christianity.

The early church rejected outright any book written under a pseudonym; that is, someone using the name of an apostle to gain credibility. The apostle Paul was already aware of such writings in his day and wrote, "We ask you, brothers, not to become easily unsettled or alarmed by some prophecy, report or letter supposed to have come from us, saying that the day of the Lord has already come" (2 Thessalonians 2:1-2). Even at that time, heretics were already writing letters signed with Paul's name. Such deceptions are inconsistent with the divine inspiration credited to the New Testament documents.

One of the reasons some rejected the book of Second Peter in the early centuries is that there were doubts as to whether Peter was indeed the author.

This is not the place to discuss the reasons for the early controversy, except to say that Origen, in about AD 240, said the book was disputed but he did not reject it. Eusebius, whom we have already met, also placed it on a list of disputed books but included it in the canon. If it had been written by a different writer, the author would likely not have begun the letter with the salutation, "Simon Peter, a servant and apostle" (1:1). Peter would have been more likely to refer to himself using *Simon* than some other author who wanted to use Peter's name to gain wide acceptance for the book.

What is more, the doctrines of the book are in accord with the other books of the New Testament, and this agreement is an added plus for its canonicity. The personal nature of his experience also confirms that the book is written by Peter, the disciple of Jesus. History has shown the wisdom of the early church to include this book in our canon. No book would have been accepted within the sacred canon if its authorship was known to be spurious.

We'd agree, I think, that any writer who attributes his writings to someone more famous in order to get acceptance is suspect. I do not agree with John Dominic Crossan of DePaul University, who in a recent television special said that this was simply an accepted procedure to reach a wider audience, implying that it was not unethical for the writers to use a well-known pseudonym.[6] That might be acceptable for the Gnostics, but if the Bible is God's Word—as many of us are convinced it is—such inspired Scripture can hardly approve of deception, even if it was a common practice.

In the Old Testament we read, "The words of the Lord are *pure* words; as silver tried in a furnace on the earth, refined seven times" (Psalm 12:6, NASB, emphasis added). And Paul in the New Testament wrote, "And we also thank God continually because, when you received the word of God, which you heard from us, you accepted it not as the word of men, but as it actually is, the word of God, which is at work in you who believe" (1 Thessalonians 2:13). That this Word of God would use deception is unthinkable.

THE LATE DATES OF THE BOOKS

These Gnostic writings are not eyewitness accounts of the events of the New Testament. Even scholars who want to give these documents credibility say that the very earliest date is about AD 150, at least one hundred or, more likely, one hundred and fifty years after the time of Jesus' crucifixion. As mentioned, other writings have been attributed to the fourth, fifth, or even sixth centuries, many hundreds of years after the time of Jesus.

Each book in *The Gnostic Bible* includes a brief introduction by a contemporary scholar. Although we are told that *The Gospel of Thomas* might have been written in the first century (other scholars believe it is much later), we learn that *The Gospel of Philip* was probably "written in the third century and possibly in Syria."[7] *The Gospel of Mary* is said probably to have been composed in the second century.[8] The point is this: Some of these gospels were written centuries after Jesus' crucifixion. Contrast this with the canonical Gospels, written by eyewitnesses and completed before AD 70 (though the Gospel of John might have been as late as AD 95).

WHAT IS GNOSTICISM?

The word *Gnostic* comes from the Greek *gnosis*, which means knowledge. More precisely, the word is used to refer to hidden knowledge that is available only to the enlightened. Gnosticism says our real need is not for forgiveness but for self-enlightenment. The Gnostics taught that Jesus can help us, but he is not necessary to our quest for salvation. Gnostics either denied the historicity of the New Testament Gospels or considered them unimportant. For them, the immediate experience of Christ mattered, not the events of his earthly activities.

If you had a choice, whose descriptions of Abraham Lincoln would you believe? Those of his contemporaries or those of people speculating about his private life or political philosophy one hundred and fifty years after his death—especially if these speculators were determined to put their own political theories into Lincoln's mouth?

THE CONTENT OF THE BOOKS

If you read the Gnostic Gospels, you will not be impressed by their similarity to the New Testament but rather by their striking differences. These gospels are nonhistorical, even *anti*historical; they contain little narrative and have no sense of chronology. They show no interest in research, geography, or historical contexts. These documents make no serious pretense of actually overlapping with the canonical Gospels. They contain some New Testament allusions to and quotations of Jesus, along with many foolish sayings that are attributed to him.

In order to get the flavor of some of these books, consider these sayings of Jesus found in the most famous of the Gnostic Gospels, *The Gospel of Thomas:*

Jesus [Yeshua] said, "Blessings on the lion if a human eats it, making the lion human. Foul is the human if a lion eats it, making the lion human."

Jesus [Yeshua] said unto them, "When you make the two into one, and when you make the inner like the outer and the outer like the inner, and the upper like the lower, and when you make the male and female into a single one, so that the male will not be the male nor the female be female, when you make eyes in the place of an eye, a hand in the place of a hand, a foot in the place of a foot, an im-

age in the place of an image, then you will enter the Kingdom."

Jesus [Yeshua] said, "Whoever has come to know the world has discovered a carcass, and whoever has discovered a carcass, of that person the world is not worthy."[9]

Sounds just like Jesus, doesn't it?

These Gnostic Gospels contain speculative ideas, most of which could have been constructed independently from the coming of Jesus Christ. Many of the sayings in *The Gospel of Thomas,* for example, could have been said by any religious leader or supposed prophet. But the Gnostics sought to tie their teachings to Jesus and the apostles to give their speculations legitimacy. Therefore, they borrowed some sayings of Jesus but largely ignored his work of redemption. Ideas, not events, mattered.

It is simply not true, as some have said, that Gnosticism represents the authentic early Christian movement that was later hijacked by the early church leaders—such as Constantine—who insisted on their own version of Christianity for political reasons. The idea that Jesus intended Mary Magdalene to be the head of the church and that the divine feminine be worshipped, but that his intentions were suppressed by power-hungry, doctrine-loving, sex-hating church officials is contradicted by dozens of verifiable early documents as will be shown later in this book.

Far from being the authentic version of Christianity, Gnosticism was a parasite that attempted to tie its platonic ideas to the fledgling but popular Christian movement. We have every reason to believe that the early church was right in insisting that Gnosticism was a corruption of the original truth and not an independently legitimate source of information about Jesus and the Christian faith. The contemporary notion that the Gnostics were the early underdogs of Christianity but were co-opted by a power-hungry church simply is not true.

In chapter 6, we'll examine in more detail how Gnosticism cannot be reconciled with historic Christianity, but rather represents an entirely different approach to the religious quest. Here it is sufficient to note that the New Testament documents stress not merely what Jesus taught but most assuredly what Jesus *did*. He came not just to teach but more importantly to die on the cross to make a personal sacrifice for sinners and then rise

ARE THE GNOSTIC GOSPELS LINKED TO THE CATHOLIC APOCRYPHA?

Not at all. The Apocrypha are books found in the Catholic Bible but not the Protestant Scriptures. These books were, for the most part, written before the time of Christ. We don't have time or space to discuss whether they are inspired Scripture, only to point out that they are not related to the Gnostic writings.

on the third day to confirm his claims. In other words, Christianity is a historical religion, rooted in certain verifiable facts. Gnosticism is a theory of ideas—conflicting ideas, I might add—that are not grounded in space/time events.

By the way, don't confuse the Gnostic Gospels with what we call the Apocrypha, the books that are found in the Catholic Bible but not the Protestant Scriptures. These additional books were, for the most part, written before the time of Christ and gained credibility when Jerome included them in the Vulgate, the Latin version of the Scriptures. We don't have time or space to discuss whether they are inspired Scripture, only to point out that they are not related to the Gnostic writings.

VERSIONS OF HISTORY

We could spend more time surveying the Gnostic Gospels, and we will discuss them again in the next chapter. For now, we must ask: Why is there a growing desire to accept these writings? We live in a postmodern age when some historians say that history should no longer be the quest to find objective facts and then, as best we can, interpret them. History, they say, should be revised to bolster self-esteem and to foster politically correct agendas.

Given this mind-set, history can be pressed into any shape one wishes in order to achieve desirable goals. The records of the past are to be deconstructed, edited, and changed to keep with the times. That's why one postmodern writer said that we must get society to react to the "imagined history of the past."[10] In other words, the attempt to discover facts should be abandoned in favor of history that has psychological value.

In *The Da Vinci Code,* Grail expert Sir Leigh Teabing said that "history is always written by the winners. When two cultures clash, the loser is obliterated, and the winner writes the history books—books which glorify their own cause and disparage the conquered foe. As Napoleon once said, 'What is history, but a fable agreed upon?'"[11] If Napoleon is right, then of course it follows that historical research is both unnecessary and counterproductive. In such a world, fiction becomes history. All we have to do is to find a fable we agree upon and run with it.

This rush to accept the Gnostic Gospels is not based on sober historical research but on a prior commitment to feminism and the desire to have a Jesus who is more like us. And of course, the notion that a divine encounter is achieved through sexual ecstasy fits right into our modern age of sexual obsession. It is a fable some have chosen to embrace.

The noted New Testament scholar Raymond Brown (no relationship to Dan Brown) said that from these gospels "we learn not a single verifiable new fact about the historical Jesus' ministry, and only a few new sayings that might possibly have been his."[12]

Catholic writer Andrew Greeley said this about *The Da Vinci Code:* "All of this is rich material, guaranteed to keep one turning pages till the story is finished. Still, the reader must wonder how much of it is fantasy. The answer, I would argue, is that practically all of it is fantasy. Every couple of years a book comes along that promises to tell you who Jesus really was and/or how the church has hidden the 'real' Jesus for 19 centuries. Somehow they do not stand up to serious historical examination."[13]

MEET A HISTORIAN

When we open our New Testament, we are struck by its *dis*similarity to the Gnostic Gospels; quite literally the difference is one of darkness and light. For example, the writer Luke gave us the methodology used in doing his historical work. He mapped out what historians used to do when facts mattered.

As you read the Bible you will discover that the Word of God came down to us in different ways. Sometimes God spoke to the prophets directly, revealing things that could not be known in any other way. Sometimes God wrote the words himself, as in the Ten Commandments. However, God also used natural means, as in the case of Luke, whose book was written after painstaking research.

In the opening paragraph, Luke explained how his book came about:

Many have undertaken to draw up an account of the things that have been fulfilled among us, just as they were handed down to us by those who from the first were eye-witnesses and servants of the word. Therefore, since I my-self have carefully investigated everything from the beginning, it seemed good also to me to write an orderly account for you, most excellent Theophilus, so that you may know the certainty of the things you have been taught. LUKE 1:1-4

Luke conducted a *careful investigation*. It's as if he said, "I am writing the greatest story in the world and it deserves the best research I can possibly give it." Though others had written about Christ and Luke does not discount their accounts—indeed, he might have benefited from their research—he determined to write with great care and attention to detail.

How did he do his research? First, he mentioned existing sources and documents that he used. But he wanted to write his own account of Jesus, because every great life deserves more than one biography. He referred to eyewitnesses who were available to verify the details. Luke was a doctor, so it stands to reason that he would have actually spoken to the Virgin Mary about the birth of Jesus.

Luke was a companion of Mark and later of the apostle Paul, so he could ask questions for clarification and verification. Because he says there were other eyewitnesses who were there "from the beginning," Luke was in a position to research the whole story.

When he said he checked out the facts accurately (from the Greek word *akribos*), he means that he kept before him the exactness of the task. The good historian does not approach his story with his mind made up; he does not begin determined to have the story come out according to his liking. He follows the facts wherever they lead.

Next, Luke *organized his material according to certain features.* He said he wanted to write an "orderly account" of the events. His organization was not always chronological; sometimes he organized his material according to various themes. Sometimes he grouped events together to make the material more understandable. He followed the chronology in a general way, putting together what belongs together so that his friend Theophilus could better understand it. Most importantly, there is rhyme and reason in his account; there is a logical progression.

Finally, he wrote *so that a reader could make an intelligent decision based on the material*. We don't know much about Theophilus (the name means "lover of God"), but evidently he was quite prominent since Luke refers to him as "most excellent Theophilus." We are grateful that Luke wrote to him and, in effect, to all of us about the wonderful story of Christ.

To his friend he wrote his intention "that you may know the certainty of the things you have been taught." He wrote openly; he knew that what his friend needed is *certainty* (the Greek word *asphaleia*). Literally, the Greek word means that "one is able to stand on a firm place" and not trip up in these matters of incredible importance. He wrote to dispel the questions Theophilus had, for at this point the man might not yet have been a Christian.

Could Luke be an unbiased historian? Of course. Did he have deep convictions about what he wrote? Yes. Does that disqualify him? Not any more than a survivor of the Holocaust is disqualified because he writes with conviction and the desire to inform people about important matters.

So how accurate a historian was Luke? He also wrote the book of Acts, which is filled with historical details: cities, seas, ships, and geographical minutiae. Sir William Ramsey, a noted nineteenth-century historian and archaeologist, set out to prove that Luke's history was filled with errors. But after a lifetime of painstaking study and work, he wrote, "Luke's history is unsurpassed in respect of its trustworthiness."[14] That assessment is confirmed by modern archaeologists as well.

THE CHOICE WE FACE

Why would anyone accept the Gnostic Gospels rather than the verifiable accounts of the canonical Scriptures? The answer can only be found in the spirit of the times: the desire for doctrinal diversity, the pressure of feminism, and the dogged insistence that we can have our own direct experience of God without the mediation of Christ. Only this desire to be "trendier than thou" can explain the mindless rush to embrace the convoluted teachings of The Gnostic Bible.

If the historicity of the New Testament was no better than that of the Gnostic Gospels, all attempts to defend the Christian faith would have collapsed long ago. *Time* magazine is right when it says, "The recovered texts also feed America's ever sharpening appetite for mystical spirituality."[15] People are seeking a relationship with God that is not tied to doctrine or formal religion. They are looking for alternate Christianities that combine a reinterpretation of Jesus with esoteric insights and the best of other religions.

Elaine Pagels, who wrote a book summarizing the teachings of the Gnostic Gospels, admits that these writings are attractive to the spiritual seeker because "in them are echoes of Buddhism and Freud with a greater appreciation of women's roles."[16] Through these documents she claims to have found a "Christianity less keyed to make-or-break beliefs like the virgin birth or even Christ's divinity and more accepting of salvation through ongoing spiritual experience."[17]

The Jesus of *The Da Vinci Code* is not a savior; he has been relegated to the role of a man—perhaps a remarkable man—but a man nonetheless. According to the Gnostics, he is one emanation from

God among many others. But in the New Testament we are confronted with an entirely different portrait of a divine man who is qualified to bridge the gap between God and us.

In chapter 6 we'll return to Gnosticism to show why it cannot be classified as a different way of being Christian. The Gnostic Jesus and the Jesus of the New Testament are radically different. And our eternal destiny depends on a proper distinction.

Enter through the narrow gate. For wide is the gate and broad is the road that leads to destruction, and many enter through it. But small is the gate and narrow is the road that leads to life, and only a few find it. MATTHEW *7:13-14*

THREE

The Da Vinci Code is so named because of the claim that Leonardo da Vinci was a member of the Priory of Sion. The Priory was a small band of conspirators who knew the truth about the marriage of Jesus and Mary Magdalene, but because of opposition from the church, this explosive secret had to be hidden. To escape the wrath of the Vatican, members of the Priory would encrypt their cherished knowledge in paintings, writings, and architecture in such a way that only the learned could decipher their meanings. Of course, in the novel the powerful Catholic organization Opus Dei is committed to intimidating the Priory in an effort to suppress the facts that would destroy Christianity as we know it.

And so in Da Vinci's paintings, the argument goes, we find hidden messages. In fact, encoded into his paintings is proof that Da Vinci knew that Jesus was married to Mary Magdalene and that she, and not a cup, was the Holy Grail. In the novel we read that "the marriage of Jesus and Mary Magdalene is part of the historical record."[1]

But is it?

In this chapter we will answer that question by discussing a series of other questions: Did Leonardo paint Mary Magdalene instead of John into his masterpiece *The Last Supper*? Is Mary herself the Holy Grail? What about the historical evidence that links the two in a special relationship? And finally, would it have been possible for Jesus to have been married?

LEONARDO, THE LAST SUPPER, AND MARY

Leonardo was an illegitimate child who, according to his grandfather's diary, was born on Saturday, April 15, 1452, in Vinci, a village some twenty miles west of Florence. (Hence "Da Vinci" is not his last name but a reference to the village in which he was born.) This precocious lad was brought to Florence where he became an apprentice to one of the master painters. Leonardo was motivated to work from dawn to dusk learning his trade. Not surprisingly, he was convinced that painting was the highest human calling, and he believed one must paint "all that the eye can see." In addition, he spent his spare time designing drills, hoists, and military equipment. He was not interested in religion, except as a vehicle for his artistic expressions.

Because he did not think his mentor in Florence appreciated him enough, Leonardo appealed to Lodovico, the duke of Milan, asking if his services might not benefit the duke. It was there that Leonardo spent twenty years of his life. In 1495, Lodovico commissioned Leonardo to do a painting of the Last Supper for the refectory of a Dominican monastery in the city of Santa Maria delle Grazie so that the friars would have something pleasing to look at while they ate.

In the novel, we are told that Leonardo, who was in on the secret, actually painted Mary Magdalene, not John, to the right of Jesus in his portrayal of the Last Supper. What is more, there is no cup on the table, because Leonardo wanted people to understand that Mary is the cup, the Holy Grail. Robert Langdon, one of the primary characters in the novel, says that Mary's presence in the painting represents "the sacred feminine and the goddess, which of course has now been lost, virtually eliminated by the Church."[2]

In his book *Humanists and Reformers: A History of the Renaissance and Reformation,* Bard Thompson said that Da Vinci's painting is a work of psychological insight, because he was not interested in doctrines, such as the sacrament. Rather, Leonardo was interested in the shock of Judas's betrayal. As we look at the painting we can see the stunned expression on the face of the disciples after Jesus announced that one of them would betray him. Judas is the only one who does not need to be told; he recoils in darkness, eating nervously.[3]

If it has been awhile since you have seen a reproduction of *The Last Supper,* find a copy and you will agree that John, sitting to the right of Jesus, does look effeminate. But Bruce Boucher of the Art Institute in Chicago disputes Dan Brown's interpretation and called it "quite a stretch. . . . Leonardo's composition points, in fact, in another direction for it confirms the traditional Florentine depic-

DOES DA VINCI'S *THE LAST SUPPER* SHOW MARY, NOT JOHN, AT THE TABLE?

The notion that Mary Magdalene rather than the apostle John is seated to the right of Jesus is rejected by most art historians. And Dan Brown's assertion that the cup is missing because Mary Magdalene is the Holy Grail misses the point that this is a work of psychological insight. Da Vinci was not interested in the sacrament, but in the shock of Judas's betrayal. When you look at the picture, you might agree that John, sitting to the right of Jesus, looks effeminate, but such a depiction was consistent with other portraits of him in Florence.

tions of the Last Supper, stressing the betrayal and sacrifice rather than the institution of the Eucharist and chalice."[4] He added that this depiction of John was consistent with other such portraits of him in Florence. Perhaps we could add that the figure has no hint of breasts. Jack Wasserman, retired art history professor at Temple University, said simply, "Just about everything [Dan Brown] says about Leonardo is wrong."[5]

But this leads us to explore the question: What was the search for the Holy Grail and what is the evidence that Mary Magdalene is the chalice, the cup that holds the blood of Christ?

THE SEARCH FOR THE HOLY GRAIL

No one knows what happened to the cup from which Jesus drank on the night he instituted the Lord's Supper. Legend says it was given to Joseph of Arimathea, but we can't be sure. What we do know is that in the twelfth century, stories circulated about the cup, which was dubbed the Holy Grail and believed to have magical power.

These legends were actually based on Celtic superstitions about the vessel as a symbol of spiritual transformation and renewal. In fact, many of these legends can be found in Greek mythology predating the time of Christ. Certain bowls or cauldrons were thought to contain hidden knowledge and spiritual benefit to those who owned them. Thus, they became associated with divination and various occult practices.

These legends were incorporated into the stories of King Arthur and the Knights of the Round Table. One account says that the Grail actually appeared, casting a spell over all who were present. King Arthur vowed that he'd find it with the help

WHAT ARE THE LEGENDS OF THE HOLY GRAIL?

Jesus drank from a cup on the night he instituted the Lord's Supper, but no one knows what happened to it. What we do know is that in the twelfth century, stories circulated about the cup, which was dubbed the Holy Grail and believed to have magical power.

In about the fifteenth century the idea developed that the Grail is not an object, but rather a family tree. Specifically, in *The Da Vinci Code,* the Grail is said to be the *Sang Real*—the royal bloodline of Jesus.

of his knights. Lancelot was the bravest, but unfortunately he loved King Arthur's wife. Because of his sin, Lancelot only saw glimpses of the Grail. Since it would appear only to those who were most pure, it eluded him and all others who sought it. Historically, any number of cups have been believed to be the sacred vessel.

For many centuries, the Grail was believed to be an object—specifically the cup or chalice used at the Last Supper. But in about the fifteenth century the idea developed that the Grail is not an object but rather a family tree. Specifically, in *The Da Vinci*

Code, the Grail is said to be the *Sang Real*—the royal bloodline of Jesus. Apparently, Mary Magdalene continued the bloodline of Jesus by bearing his child. One of Jesus' descendants created the Merovingian line of French royalty. The novel ends with the main character at the Louvre's inverted pyramid in Paris, praying at what could be Mary's tomb. One of the final lines is "The quest for the Holy Grail is the quest to kneel before the bones of Mary Magdalene. A journey to pray at the feet of the outcast one."[6] This would have surprised the knights who sought the Holy Grail, believing it to be a chalice.

But is there reasonable evidence that Mary might have been married to Jesus? She is mentioned in passages from the Gnostic Gospels that were introduced in the last chapter. As we know, the Bible does speak about her relationship with Jesus. She is the first witness to the Resurrection and was known by some in the church as "the apostle of the Apostles."

So, who was Mary Magdalene? Let's discover what the New Testament says about her, and then we will consider the references to her in the Gnostic Gospels.

MARY MAGDALENE AND THE NEW TESTAMENT

New Testament writer Luke introduces us to a group of women who followed Jesus and the disciples, helping to support them financially. Some of these women "had been cured of evil spirits and diseases: Mary (called Magdalene) from whom seven demons had come out; Joanna the wife of Cuza, the manager of Herod's household; Susanna; and many others. These women were helping to support them out of their own means" (Luke 8:2-3).

We should pause long enough to reflect that this passage shows that Jesus broke with tradition in allowing women to travel with him and help support his ministry. The rabbis of the day would not have tolerated such openness toward women nor the honor that came with such direct association. Women were usually identified by their husbands, but Mary is called Magdalene; she is identified by where she was from (Magdala was situated on the western shores of Galilee). Possibly she was unmarried.

The previous chapter in Luke includes a story of an unnamed prostitute who came to Jesus, and some have speculated that she was Mary Magdalene. In AD 591, Pope Gregory the Great gave an

Easter sermon in which he declared that the prostitute of Luke 7 was Mary Magdalene who is mentioned in Luke 8. But there really is no reason to make such a connection.

Perhaps Pope Gregory's speculative identification was intended to repress any legends about Mary's role in the early church. But it is a stretch to assume that she was branded a prostitute in order to suppress her supposed rivalry with the apostle Peter. The argument of *The Da Vinci Code* is that Jesus intended the church to be built on Mary, but that the early church doctored documents and declared her a harlot to render her unfit for such a high office. At any rate, in 1969 the Vatican rightly corrected centuries of misrepresentation and acknowledged that there was no reason to make Mary a repentant harlot.

Sometimes Mary Magdalene also has been mistakenly identified as Mary of Bethany, the sister of Martha and Lazarus. But there is no doubt that she is called Mary *Magdalene* for the express purpose of distinguishing her from the other Marys in the Gospels. Of this we can be certain: She had a marvelous story of conversion and was the first witness to the resurrection of the Lord she loved.

Mary's ministry to Jesus brought her in contact with Salome, the mother of James and John, and also with Mary, the mother of our Lord (John 19:25). These brave women were standing at the foot of the cross when Jesus died. Mary Magdalene kept watch until the body was taken down and wrapped in linen and placed in the tomb of Joseph of Arimathea (Matthew 27:61; Mark 15:47; Luke 23:55).

Then on the first day of the week, she and the other women "bought spices so that they might go to anoint" the body (Mark 16:1). When they arrived, they found the tomb empty and saw an angel who told them that Jesus had been raised from the dead. Mary went to tell Peter and John the news and returned with them to the tomb. Though it was empty, Jesus could not be found, so Mary stayed there even after the two men left.

Looking into the tomb, she saw angels, who asked her why she was weeping. She replied, "They have taken my Lord away, and I don't know where they have put him"(John 20:13).

She peered into the dark tomb long enough to be satisfied that it was empty. One has to imagine that she was contemplating what to do next.

Slowly she backed away and straightened herself, her eyes adjusting to the light around her.

At this, she turned around and saw Jesus standing there, but she did not realize that it was Jesus.

"Woman," he said, "Why are you crying? Who is it you are looking for?"

Thinking he was the gardener, she said, "Sir, if you have carried him away, tell me where you have put him, and I will get him."

Jesus said to her, "Mary!"

She turned toward him and cried out . . . , "Rabboni!" (which means Teacher).

Jesus said to her, "Do not hold on to me, for I have not yet returned to the Father. Go instead to my brothers and tell them, 'I am returning to my Father and your Father, to my God and your God.'"

JOHN 20:14-17

Mary Magdalene wanted to cling to Jesus' feet like a child who fears the departure of a parent. Now that she had found him, she did not want to lose him.

But for now, Jesus said, "Don't do that."

Jesus was in effect saying to Mary, "You will see

me again, for I have not yet ascended to my Father. Don't think you will lose me, because I will be with you for the next forty days. No need to panic." Yes, it was the same Jesus, but the nature of the relationship was changed.

In defense of *The Da Vinci Code,* some argue that taboos about a woman touching a man existed in those days, so this account implies that she and Jesus were married. But undoubtedly this was a spontaneous act of devotion. Most assuredly Jesus could be touched, for later when the women left the tomb, he met them and we read, "And they came up and took hold of His feet and worshiped Him" (Matthew 28:9, NASB). Obviously, Mary wasn't the only woman allowed to touch Jesus. Our Savior was not restricted by cultural customs that would hinder a woman to appropriately touch a man.

Mary no doubt had a deep love for Jesus, but there is no hint of romance between them. She was indeed an honored and privileged woman to have attracted the loving mercy of the Savior. And we can be glad that all who come to Jesus are similarly accepted. After the story of the Resurrection, Mary passes from the pages of the New Testament only to resurface centuries later in the mythology of occult teachings and New Age agendas.

I agree that historically the church can be faulted for not giving women their rightful place in Christian ministry. However, we must reject *The Da Vinci Code*'s claims that "Jesus was the original feminist" because of the meaning of that phrase in today's society. Jesus *did* reject those cultural taboos that put women in a disrespected place as second-class citizens of the Kingdom. Women in Scripture are equal with men, though their roles are different.

WAS JESUS REALLY MARRIED TO, OR IN A RELATIONSHIP WITH, MARY MAGDALENE?

We know of no eyewitness documents that would give evidence of the marriage of Jesus to Mary. She no doubt had a deep love for Jesus, but in the most reliable accounts, there is no hint of romance between them. Women were usually identified by their husbands, but Mary is called Magdalene; she is identified by where she was from. Possibly she was unmarried. Even if the accounts from the Gnostic Gospels were accurate, it would be a stretch to say that Mary had a romantic relationship with Jesus, much less that they were married.

Needless to say, this is not the place to enter into current debates about the place of women in the church, except to emphasize that Jesus broke the mold, elevating women to a place of respect and honor. The fact that he talked with the immoral woman while alone at Jacob's well and that women such as Mary Magdalene were invited to travel with him shows that he was willing to discard the taboos and invite women into his sphere of influence.

MARY MAGDALENE AND THE GNOSTIC GOSPELS

In *The Da Vinci Code* we are told that in concealing the truth about Jesus' marriage to Mary, the church has engaged in the "greatest cover-up in human history." Evidence for their marriage is supposedly found in the Gnostic Gospels. We've already learned that these gospels are misnamed, for in reality they are not "gospels" at all. Nevertheless, we must consider what they have to say about Jesus and Mary Magdalene.

First, *The Gospel of Philip* says:

The companion is Mary of Magdala. Jesus loved her more than his students. He kissed her often on her face, more than all his students, and they said, "Why do you love her more than us?" The savior answered, saying to them, "Why do I not love you like her? If a blind man and one who sees are together in darkness, they are the same. When light comes, the one who sees will see light. The blind man stays in darkness."[7]

You should know that because of the poor quality of the papyrus, a word or two is missing in the original. The text reads, "Jesus kissed her often on the [blank] . . ." So scholars fill in the blank with the word *mouth*, *face*, or *forehead*, etc. Actually, for all we know the text might have said "the hand" or even "the cheek" since the statement implies that he also kissed his other students—presumably on the cheek as is still done in the Middle East.

The account, even if true, says nothing about marriage. But *The Da Vinci Code* makes the claim, "As any Aramaic scholar will tell you, the word *companion*, in those days, literally meant *spouse*."[8] Of course, we should point out that this account did not come down to us in Aramaic, but Coptic. For another, the word *companion* in either language is frequently used for friendship; by no means does it always mean marriage.

Is this account even credible? Before we answer, we should remind ourselves that *The Gospel of Philip* is dated by scholars as written in about the third century, about two hundred years after the time of Jesus—not exactly an eyewitness account!

Read this gospel and you will find it to be a rambling and disjointed work with abrupt changes in subject matter. It includes such teachings as "there are many animals that exist in the world which are in human form." It also says "Winter is the world, summer the other realm. It is wrong to pray in winter." And if you want more wisdom, consider this:

God is a dyer.
The good dyes, true dyes, dissolve into things
Dyed in them.
So too for things god has dyed.
His dyes are imperishable because of their colors.
What god dips, he dips in water.[9]

The Gnostics believed in two gods and the creating god was evil. We read: "The world came into being through error. The agent who made it wanted it to be imperishable and immortal. He failed."[10] In the rest of the book, Jesus is presented as one among many beings that emanated from God. These kinds of texts are clearly intended to articulate a pagan philosophy, not to say something credible about Jesus. You can write anything you want if you are not concerned about facts.

Remember, we don't have a clue as to who wrote this gospel. Most assuredly it was not Philip of the New Testament but some pseudo-author who cobbled together a plethora of disjointed Gnostic ideas. Perhaps he wrote what he did because legends about Mary Magdalene were already circulating by the third century. At any rate, this unknown author could only speculate about Jesus' relationship with Mary. And, apparently, he used these speculations for his own purposes.

In the Gnostic *Gospel of Mary,* Mary Magdalene is described as having a special revelation given to her by the Savior. At Peter's request, she tells the other disciples about a vision she had with Jesus and how she asked him whether one sees a vision through the soul or through the spirit. The Savior answered, "A person sees neither through the soul nor the spirit. The mind, which lives between the two, sees the vision."

After some rather esoteric explanations about

the soul, Peter asked, "Did he really speak to a woman secretly, without our knowledge and not openly? Are we to turn and all listen to her? Did he prefer her to us?" Mary began to weep and assured Peter that she did not make this up herself.

At this point, Levi stepped into the conversation and said, "Peter, you are always angry. Now I see you contending against this woman as if against an adversary. If the savior made her worthy, who are you to reject her? Surely the savior knows her very well. That is why he loved her more than us."[11] Then the disciples are admonished to go out and preach, which they do.

This story is another attempt by the Gnostics to give legitimacy to their esoteric doctrines of knowledge for the inner circle of the initiated. This account was likely included for two reasons: first, to make the point that women should be able to preach, and second, that private revelations from God have the same status as the teachings of bishops. Mary Magdalene, who figures prominently in the canonical Gospels as the first witness to the Resurrection, would be the natural choice for this dialogue.

Even if these accounts from the Gnostic Gospels

were accurate, it is a stretch to say that Mary had a romantic relationship with Jesus, much less that she was married to him. At this point as in so many others, *The Da Vinci Code* bases its conclusions on imaginary data, hoping that gullible readers will give them credence.

Much controversy surrounds the Priory of Sion, which was evidently founded in 1099. Although we don't know what legends were circulating at the time, we know of no eyewitness documents that would give evidence of the marriage of Jesus and Mary. And it is unlikely that Opus Dei, begun in 1928, had anything to do with applying pressure to the Priory to keep a lid on its secret. As a novel, it works; as history, it is a house of cards that can be toppled by the slightest breath of truth.

MARY AND THE LEGENDS

The Templar Revelation argues in detail that Jesus and Mary were married, or at least that they were sexual partners. In writing their book, the authors toured the Magdalene shrines of southern France where legends about her arose in about the ninth century. The purpose of their book is to evaluate this folklore and argue for its plausibility. In the process, they aim to destroy the traditional teaching about Jesus as found in the New Testament.

In their travels the authors discovered that legends about Mary Magdalene are linked with the pagan goddess Isis and the mother-child cult associated with Mary, the mother of Jesus. What is more, wherever there are Magdalene centers there are also shrines and myths about John the Baptist. The authors argue that John actually did not put himself under the authority of Jesus as the New Testament claims; rather, Jesus was a disciple of John. And John's anointed successor was actually the Gnostic sex magician Simon Magnus, who is mentioned in the book of Acts (8:9-25)!

If you've still not heard enough, it might surprise you to learn that some claim Jesus, John the Baptist, and Mary Magdalene all had "Gnostic awareness of the Divine," baptizing people and thus initiating them into "the ancient occult tradition." The miracles of Simon Magnus, like those of Jesus, were an intrinsic part of this religious practice. "Ritual was central to this movement, from the first baptism to the enactment of the Egyptian mysteries. But the supreme initiation came through sexual ecstasy."[12]

If you are wondering about the authors' sources,

understand that they have taken all of the legends and occult practices of ancient times and interpreted the New Testament accounts in light of these esoteric mythologies. Thus, we should not be surprised that Jesus himself turns out to be the son of a goddess and that the anointing by Mary of Bethany (the authors believe she is Mary Magdalene) was a sexual ritual performed by a priestess. "The anointing of Jesus was a pagan ritual: the woman who performed it—Mary of Bethany—was a priestess. Given this new scenario it is more than likely that her role in Jesus' inner circle was as a sexual initiatrix."[13]

All Christians should be appalled by these allegations! But once mythologies are given the status of history and imaginary dots are connected between unrelated events, any spin can be imposed upon the records of the past. Then one can go on to say that the reason the real "truth" was banned from the Bible was that the church has always championed sexual repression and the degrading of women. The power-hungry, money-loving church has always stood in favor of male supremacy and rigid control, thus rejecting out of hand the divine feminine.

How incredible that occult writers should so

twist the New Testament as to make it an occult document! The very writings that call us to a life of holiness and purity are pressed into service to affirm an immoral pagan agenda. Imagine the Jesus who said "anyone who looks at a woman lustfully has already committed adultery with her in his heart" (Matthew 5:28) approving and evidently participating in an occult sex ritual!

Keep in mind that sex rituals have always been practiced in pagan religion, whether in ancient or modern times. But the notion that this is the way to holiness or that through such encounters we connect with God is exactly the kind of teaching that Jesus and the New Testament writers debunk. They warn against such practices, which violate the sanctity of marriage and the moral purity expected of Christians. "For of this you can be sure: No immoral, impure or greedy person—such a man is an idolater—has any inheritance in the kingdom of Christ and of God. Let no one deceive you with empty words" (Ephesians 5:5-6). As we shall see in a later chapter, we connect with God spiritually through Christ, not through sexual ecstasy.

We can understand why in the second century Irenaeus, commenting about how the Gnostics used the Bible in his day, said that Gnosticism is like taking a beautiful picture of a king and reassembling it to become a picture of a fox. No wonder Peter, speaking of false teachers, wrote, "Many will follow their shameful ways and will bring the way of truth into disrepute. In their greed these teachers will exploit you with stories they have made up" (2 Peter 2:2-3).

As it was then, so it is today!

JESUS AND MARRIAGE

Could Jesus have been married?

Dan Brown says in Jesus' day it was rare for a man not to be married. And he claims since Jesus was human, he would have desired sexual inti-

WOULDN'T IT HAVE BEEN CONTRARY TO CUSTOM FOR JESUS TO BE SINGLE?

Although Jewish rabbis were usually married, there was no requirement that they be married. Also, although Jesus was called rabbi, he was not a part of the rabbinical order of his day. New Testament writers such as Matthew and John who knew him best make no reference to his marriage, which, had it occurred, would certainly have been mentioned.

macy and female companionship. This, however, does not provide evidence that Jesus was married. We do know that New Testament writers such as Matthew and John, who knew Jesus best, make no reference to his marriage, which, had it occurred, would certainly have been mentioned.

We might speculate that Jesus could have been married, since marriage is "honorable and unde-filed." Since he was a human being—indeed even a sinless human being—we can assume he could have married. However, because he had both a human nature and a divine nature we must confess it is un-thinkable that Jesus, the God-man, could be joined to a sinner in the most intimate physical human bond. If he had married, presumably it would have been to someone as holy as he—which severely limited his options!

Of course, someday Jesus will be married. We all anticipate his future wedding. Jesus is now engaged to us, the church—his bride. He would not have been married on earth, knowing that his coming marriage is in heaven. On that day, we, along with Mary Magdalene, will be invited to the marriage supper of the Lamb, where the marriage is consummated, not in a physical sexual union, but in the most blessed

and intimate union of fellowship imaginable. Yes,
Jesus will be married—not to a woman—but to all of
us who constitute the bride of Christ.

*"Let us rejoice and be glad and give him glory! For the
wedding of the Lamb has come, and his bride has made
herself ready. Fine linen, bright and clean, was given her
to wear." (Fine linen stands for the righteous acts of the
saints.) Then the angel said to me, "Write: 'Blessed are
those who are invited to the wedding supper of the
Lamb!'"* REVELATION 19:7-9

Given this larger perspective, Jesus' obvious celi-
bacy was both necessary and proper.

The invitation to attend this wedding does not
come from the Gnostic Jesus, but rather the Jesus
who is King of kings and Lord of lords. "Therefore
God exalted him to the highest place and gave him
the name that is above every name, that at the name
of Jesus every knee should bow, in heaven and on
earth and under the earth, and every tongue confess
that Jesus Christ is Lord, to the glory of God the
Father" (Philippians 2:9-11).

Only those who accept his invitation will gather
to enjoy the feast.

FOUR

The Bible is a product of *man,* my dear. Not of God," says Sir Leigh Teabing in *The Da Vinci Code.* "The Bible did not fall magically from the clouds. Man created it as a historical record of tumultuous times, and it has evolved through countless translations, additions, and revisions. History has never had a definitive version of the book."[1]

Yes, it is true that the Bible did not fall magically from the clouds. And it is also true that man wrote the Bible in a given historical context, often in tumultuous times. But there is also powerful evidence that the Bible is more than a book written by men, that it is a book men wrote as they

were inspired by God. There is every reason to believe that the Bible gives reliable information
about all that it teaches. Such reasons are available
to those who are interested in seeking the truth.[2]

However, this chapter will take us in a slightly
different direction. Here, we'll discuss the following questions: On what basis were some books included and others excluded from the canon? Is it
true that, as *The Da Vinci Code* says, the Gnostic Gospels were banned by men who wanted to change
the church from a matriarchal to a patriarchal
community? Is it true that some books didn't make
it into the canon by an unwarranted act of censorship?

On Christmas Day 2003, the History Channel
carried a two-hour special titled *Banned from the
Bible,* a discussion of the various books that were
written at the time of the New Testament but were
excluded from the canon. The clear impression
was that some books were banned merely because
they were pro-feminine or too risqué to be included. The documentary also implied that at
least a few of these books would have made a helpful addition to the Scriptures if they had been included. Indeed, the program claimed, since the

Bible is a human book, writings were included or excluded by powerful individuals for religious and political reasons.

At this point we must clarify that there are two groups of books that were not included in the canon. One group is the Gnostic Gospels, which we have already discussed in some detail. But the History Channel primarily referred to a second group of books that have been known for centuries and are accessible to anyone who wants to read them. These are the apocryphal writings that have been known since ancient times. Again, I must point out that these books must be distinguished from the additional books found in the Catholic Bible that predate these "banned books."

Some of these "banned books" teach that:

- When Jesus was a boy, he killed a child by pushing him off a roof and, when accused, responded by using his power to raise him from the dead. In fact, Jesus apparently used his power for impish personal reasons until he grew up and only then used his divine powers to accomplish good.
- After the Fall, Adam devised a plan for Eve and him to return to the Garden of Eden by standing in different

rivers. He stood in the River Jordan for forty days and Eve, being weaker, was supposed to stand in the Tigris River for thirty-four days. But the devil appeared to her again, and she came out of the water on the eighteenth day, ruining the plan and incurring Adam's deep displeasure.

- In hell blasphemers are hung up by their tongues and fornicators by their genitals. But if people ask God for deliverance, all of hell will be emptied. However no one is to know this, because if they do, they will sin even more.

Of course, other books that are more in sync with the Bible were also not included in the canon. There were dozens of writings in circulation when the New Testament was assembled, many of them purporting to be alternate stories about Jesus. A few even vied for a position in the canon.

Banned from the Bible also implied that only after Constantine converted to Christianity was a serious effort made to compile a New Testament. And we are told it took another forty years after the Council of Nicaea for the church to canonize the complete list of twenty-seven New Testament books (AD 367). The program gave the impression that for hundreds of years the Christian church had no agreed-upon canon.

How much of this is true and how much is skewed to fit with popular notions about the nature of the Bible and the canonization process? Let's take a quick look at the books "banned" from the Bible and then discuss how the canon actually came to be.

THE BANNED BOOKS

The books that were excluded from the Bible were considered by the early church to be pseudo-epigraphical, that is, fraudulent writings that the early leaders regarded as tales hatched in fertile imaginations. History shows that legends always develop around famous figures, and we should not be surprised that some people would attach superstitions to Jesus that have no basis in fact. These are the books that contain the stories referred to earlier: stories about the infancy of Jesus, the alternate understandings about hell, and the like. Unlike the Gnostic Gospels, these legends have been known from antiquity.

The question comes down to this: Why were some books included in the canon, and why were others rejected? Most important, who made these decisions and when were these decisions made? Is it true that there was no agreed-upon canon until forty years after the time of Constantine? And should we consider the canon to be open; that is, does anyone have the right to insist that other books be included in Holy Scripture?

THE DEVELOPMENT OF THE CANON

The Bible is a remarkable collection of sixty-six books united by a common theme. Like a tapestry, it weaves together the story of God's redemption of the human race. That these books should be collected, agreed upon, and accepted as the Word of God is itself a miracle of God's providence. Sketching the big picture will help us put the details in perspective.

Many people suppose that the decision as to what books were included or excluded was made by a church council that met behind closed doors and debated the merits of each book, accepting some and rejecting others. Others surmise that these books "just happened" to be collected without any special criteria by which they would be judged worthy of Scripture. Still others think that the decision was made on the basis of a sinister act of censorship, as *The Da Vinci Code* alleges.

Let's first summarize the way the Old Testament books were collected. This will provide a pattern that will be important in discussing the collection of the New Testament books.

THE OLD TESTAMENT CANON

When God authorized the writing of a manuscript and the people of God recognized it as such, it was preserved. For example, Moses wrote "all the words of the Lord" (Exodus 24:4, KJV) and these writings were carefully laid in the ark of the covenant (Deuteronomy 31:26); so were the writings of Joshua (Joshua 24:26) and Samuel, whose words were put "in a book, and laid . . . before the Lord" (1 Samuel 10:25, KJV). The same can be said for the books of Jeremiah and Daniel (Daniel 9:2).

Obviously, the number of books increased and subsequent generations honored them as the Word of the Lord. For example, Ezra possessed a copy of the law of Moses and the prophets (Nehemiah 9:14, 26-30). This law was read and revered as the Word of God.

Not all Jewish religious literature was considered

part of the list of inspired books. For example the book of Jashar existed (Joshua 10:13), as did the Book of the Wars of the Lord (Numbers 21:14) and others (1 Kings 11:41). These books did not survive the centuries, so we don't know their content.

As the canon grew in size, it often was described with the phrase, "Moses and the prophets." Later it was referred to as "the Law, Prophets, and the Writings" (or "the Psalms"). Jesus himself alluded to this threefold division when he spoke of "the Law of Moses, and the Prophets and the Psalms" (Luke 24:44).

To be fair, we must report that the canonicity of five Old Testament books was questioned at one time or another, each for a different reason. For some, the Song of Solomon was too sensual; Ecclesiastes was too skeptical; and because Esther does not mention the name of God, some thought it too unspiritual. Some questioned Proverbs because some of the maxims seemed to contradict one another. And finally, some Jewish scholars thought Ezekiel was anti-Mosaic, and its visions were said to tend toward Gnosticism.

Despite these objections, most of the Jewish scholars did not question these books; they were regarded as canonical soon after they were written, and when properly interpreted are in complete harmony with the other books of the Old Testament. The centuries have proven the wisdom of keeping them within the biblical canon.

As far as we know, the Jews agreed that the canon of the Old Testament closed in about 400 BC with the prophecy of Malachi; indeed, the period between the Old Testament and the New Testament is often referred to as the Four Hundred Silent Years. God was not speaking directly to his people, and no words of his were written down.

What can we know for sure? First, we know that our Old Testament is based on the Hebrew Old Testament canon that was accepted by the Jews. And second, this is the same canon that Christ ratified by his frequent references to the Old Testament as the unbreakable Word of God. Because of his approval of these books, we can be confident that the Old Testament canon is authoritative and closed.[3]

In this process we see the providence of God. Remember, these Old Testament books were selected by the people of God without the benefit of a council to debate the merits of each book. The very leaders who were responsible for Israel's spiritual life determined which books belonged in the Old Testament. While they may at times have had disagreements, those decisions were never in the hands of a select committee.

Yes, a council met in Jamnia in AD 90 and the canon of the Old Testament was on its agenda, but it only ratified books that the Jews had accepted five centuries earlier. The authentic books had proved their worth; the wheat had been separated from the chaff.

THE NEW TESTAMENT CANON

The same authority we noted in the Old Testament is ascribed to the writers of the New Testament. Their authority is not found in human brilliance or speculation but is rooted in the character of God. Paul could tell the congregation in Corinth that what he was writing to them was the Lord's command (1 Corinthians 14:37).

Jesus commissioned the disciples to pass on the truth he had taught them: "All this I have spoken while still with you. But the Counselor, the Holy Spirit, whom the Father will send in my name, will teach you all things and will remind you of every-

HOW WAS THE NEW TESTAMENT PUT TOGETHER?

The books of the New Testament were written during the last half of the first century. Because of limitations of communication and travel, some time passed before the number of books regarded as authoritative was finally settled. There were several criteria for inclusion in the canon: first, apostolicity (written or sanctioned by an apostle); second, conformity to the rule of faith (consistent with the Old Testament prophets and the New Testament apostles); and third, widespread and continuous acceptance. Councils only ratified what the church had already done; *no council or pope imposed upon the churches books that they had not already accepted.*

thing I have said to you" (John 14:25-26). Of course we must realize that the early church did not have a central worship center to house the books as the Jews did. Christianity spread beyond the bounds of Judaism and became an international religion; there was no special location that served as a central base of authority. Persecution scattered the church in all directions.

The books of the New Testament were written during the last half of the first century. Most of the books were written to local churches (the majority of Paul's epistles were written to churches in cities such as Ephesus, Philippi, etc.), and some were addressed to individuals. Other books, penned by various writers, were written for a broader audience in eastern Asia (1 Peter), western Asia (Revelation), and even Europe (Romans).

With such geographical diversity of origin and destination, it is understandable that not all the churches immediately had copies of these various letters. Because of limitations of communication and travel, some time passed before the number of books regarded as authoritative was finally settled.

Obviously, a process of selection and verification was important to the early believers. And as long as the apostles were alive, everything could be checked out (Luke 1:2; Acts 1:21-22). For example, John could say, "The life appeared; we have seen it and testify to it, and we proclaim to you the eternal life, which was with the Father and has appeared to us. We proclaim to you what we have seen and heard" (1 John 1:2-3). Peter assured us that he was an eyewitness of the Transfiguration, and his description was based on firsthand evidence (2 Peter 1:16-18). Apostolic authority was a final court of appeal.

Just as books were added to the Old Testament canon, so the various books of the New Testament gained acceptance as they were written and circulated. From earliest times the church had a functional canon; that is, *some books were accepted as authoritative even when others were not yet written.*

Paul commanded the Thessalonians, "I adjure you by the Lord to have this letter read to all the brethren" (1 Thessalonians 5:27, NASB). And again to the Colossians he wrote, "When this letter is read among you, have it also read in the church of the Laodiceans" (Colossians 4:16, NASB). John promised a blessing for all who listened to the book of Revelation being read (Revelation 1:3). Clearly the apostolic letters were intended for the whole church. There was a kind of round-robin circulation of books that steadily grew.

That some books were accepted as Scripture soon after they were written can be confirmed by the words of Peter. He possessed a collection of Paul's letters and regarded them as Scripture. Listen to this amazing confirmation of Paul's authority. Peter wrote: "Regard the patience of our Lord to be salvation; just as also our beloved brother Paul, according to the wisdom given him, wrote to you, as also in all his letters, speaking in them of these things, in which are some things hard to understand, which the untaught and unstable distort, as they do also the rest of the Scriptures, to their own destruction" (2 Peter 3:15-16, NASB). Paul's letters were almost immediately regarded as authoritative Scripture.

Other books enjoyed the same acceptance. Jude 1:17-18 quoted from Peter (2 Peter 3:3); in 1 Timothy 5:18 Paul cited Luke's Gospel as Scripture (Luke 10:7). Obviously, the believers of the early church recognized a growing body of literature as the inspired Word of God. By the end of the first century more than two thirds of our present New Testament was deemed inspired. The remaining books were known and quoted as authoritative even though they had not yet achieved wide circulation.

Yes, there were some disagreements. Hebrews was suspect in the minds of some because the authorship of the book is unknown; some doubted that Second Peter was written by Peter, ascribing it to an unknown author who borrowed his material from Jude. Revelation is missing from some early lists, probably because it was unknown in some places.

When a heretic named Marcion, in opposition to the Christian writings, came out with his own version of the Scriptures in AD 135, the early church was forced to define which books would be regarded as authoritative. Marcion was fiercely anti-Jewish and opposed to biblical law. Believing that the God of the Old Testament was different from the God of the New Testament, he eliminated the Old Testament and chose only those New Testament books that suited his fancy. The church had to respond and declare what books were authoritative.

A document called the *Muratorian Fragment*, dating back to about AD 175, evaluates the various canonical books along with those that had been rejected by the church. Unfortunately, this aged document is mutilated. However, even though parts of it are missing, scholars can identify a list that contains about twenty-three of our present twenty-seven books. It also lists some forged documents ascribed to the apostle Paul. As for such spurious writings, the author noted that these books cannot be received into the catholic church "since it is not fitting that poison should be mixed with honey."[4] Such writings were not banned from the Bible; they were brushed aside because they were recognized to be forgeries.

A few books might legitimately be said to have been banned from the Bible, such as the *Shepherd of Hermes,* a book that was accepted as canonical by some churches but eventually rejected because it was written too late and its theology contradicted the other writings of the canon. The book teaches that if we add to our sins we cannot be saved and that we have only one chance at repentance. We can be grateful that the *Shepherd of Hermes* is not Scripture! Some thought that the *Epistle of Barnabas* and a document known as the *Didache* (the teaching of the apostles) should be in the canon. These and other noncanonical books were read in some churches.

THE CANON IS CLOSED

What about the contention that the New Testament list of books was not finalized until forty years after the Council of Nicaea, which took place in AD 325? It is true that the complete list of our twenty-seven accepted books first appeared in the Easter letter of Athanasius in AD 367. But—and this is important—by that time, this canon of twenty-seven books, with some variations, had already functioned as the rule of the church for more than 250 years!

In chapter 1 we learned that Constantine did not decide which books would be in the canon; indeed, the topic of the canon did not even come up at the Council of Nicaea. By that time the early church was reading a canon of books it had determined was the Word of God two hundred years earlier.

What Constantine did do, however, was commission the historian Eusebius of Caesarea to make fifty Bibles, to be copied onto good parchment by trained scribes for use in the churches of Constantinople. We wish we had a list of the books so we could verify what books of the New Testament were included in these volumes.

However, even though we do not have copies of these Bibles, there is every reason to believe that the list of books included in the New Testament was the same as our present-day canon. F. F. Bruce, who for twenty years was the Rylands Professor of Biblical Criticism and Exegesis at the University of Manchester, says that although we are not told which books of the New Testament were in those Bibles, "the answer is not seriously in doubt. The copies contained all the books which Eusebius lists as universally acknowledged . . . in short, the same twenty-seven books as appear in our copies of the New Testament today."[5] The evidence points to the conclusion that Eusebius was simply accepting those books that had been accepted by the church as inspired Scripture.

Please know that the only thing the early church could do was to recognize those books that were inspired by the Holy Spirit. No council or church could take nonauthoritative books and endow them with divine authority. A book either does or does not have inherent authority; it is either from God or it is not. A letter written by George Washington would be authentic even if historians did not recognize it as such. And if it were not written by him, all the councils and pronouncements of men could not make it become a letter from his hand. All that the early church could do was to determine whether or not a book was inspired by God.

We can be grateful that once the present twenty-seven New Testament books were accepted, no credible moves were made within the church to

WHY WERE SOME BOOKS LEFT OUT OF THE BIBLE?

Many books were circulating around the time of Jesus, and the early church had to decide which ones were authoritative. Various books had to be left out. Many of these were considered by the early church to be pseudoepigraphical; that is, fraudulent writings. The Gnostic Gospels fit this category because they were not written by the apostles as claimed. Such writings were not banned from the Bible; they were not even considered because they were recognized to be forgeries and heresies.

either delete some or add others. There are good reasons to believe that the early church correctly discerned writings that came to them from God. The results of the process were not contrived.

CRITERIA FOR ACCEPTANCE

In retrospect, what were the criteria for books to be included in the canon? First, there was *apostolicity;* that is, the book was written by an apostle or sanctioned by one. Although Mark was not one of the apostles, his teaching reflects his association with Peter; Luke traveled with Paul. This is one reason why the *Shepherd of Hermes* was rejected; it was written too late to be connected to one of the apostles.

Second, there was *conformity* to the rule of faith; that is, the book's teachings were consistent with the Old Testament prophets and the New Testament apostles. Thus, although the authorship of the book of Hebrews is unknown, it was seen as an inspired exposition of how Jesus fulfilled Old Testament law and its rituals.

Third, a document had to have widespread and continuous *acceptance* to be included. Jerome gives his own reason why it does not matter who wrote the book of Hebrews: It is the work of a "church-writer" and in harmony with the truth of the churches where it is constantly read and accepted.[6]

I can't make this point too strongly: The various books were not accepted or rejected by a council or a committee. The process was not what *The Da Vinci Code* describes as a power grab. Councils only ratified what the church had already done; *no council or pope imposed upon the churches books that the people of God had not already accepted.*

Consider the following brief sketch of how the New Testament canon came to be:

1. Letters from apostles were written and received in the churches; copies were made and circulated.

2. A growing group of books developed that were recognized as inspired Scripture. Important questions for their acceptance included: Was the book written by either an apostle or someone who knew the apostles and thus had the stamp of apostolic authority? Was it in harmony with other accepted doctrine?

3. By the end of the first century all twenty-seven books in our present canon had been written and received by the churches. Though some of the canonical lists were incomplete, this is not always to be interpreted as the rejection of some books. Often it simply means that some books were unknown in certain areas.

4. As an indication of both agreement and the widespread acceptance of the New Testament books, we should note that a generation after the end of the apostolic age, every book of the New Testament had been cited as authoritative by some church father.[7]

5. Remaining doubts or debates over certain books continued into the fourth century. It bears

repeating that as far as historians know, the first time the list of our twenty-seven books appears is in an Easter letter written by Athanasius, an outstanding leader of the church in AD 367.

6. The twenty-seven books of our New Testament were ratified by the Council of Hippo (AD 393) and the Third Council of Carthage (AD 397).

As the *New Catholic Encyclopedia* states, "The canon, already implicitly present in the apostolic age, gradually became explicit through a number of providential factors forming and fixing it."[8] The councils of the church had no knowledge or power that was not available to Christians generally. There was no politically engineered canonization process.

COULD THE CHURCH HAVE ERRED?

In this chapter, we've seen how the people of God recognized certain books as authoritative as they were written. These people were careful to observe all that the apostles taught and wrote, believing these men to be representatives of the Christ they knew in the flesh.

But could the church have erred? We believe it

was a *fallible* church that chose what we believe to be an *infallible* list of books that comprise our New Testament. Theoretically, the church could have erred, for the church is not infallible. But there is no reason to believe that it did. First, no other books make a credible claim for inclusion in the New Testament canon. The Gnostic books, such as *The Gospel of Thomas,* simply fail the tests necessary for inclusion, not the least of which is that they are out of harmony with the rule of faith. To the person who thinks the church erred, I say, "Set forth your case . . . show me what book should be included and why."

Second, a good amount of circumstantial evidence shows that God guided the process of selecting those books that the church agreed were canonical. Given the geographical distances, the limitations of communication, and the diverse backgrounds of the churches, such agreement is remarkable.

Are you still troubled at the thought that it was a fallible church that selected what we believe to be infallible Scriptures? You should not be surprised. *After all, it was fallible human beings who wrote the infallible Scriptures.* King David in the Old Testament and the apostle Peter in the New Testament are examples of writers whose sins and failures are well-known. Yet David wrote infallible psalms, and Peter, who denied Christ, wrote two infallible epistles. Just so, a fallible church could be led of God to choose an infallible list of books.

If you have doubts about whether other books should have been included, I encourage you to spend time reading the Gnostic Gospels or the so-called Lost Books of the Bible. You will discover that they are filled with hybrid teachings, superstitions, and foolish heresies. Then turn to the Scriptures and you will be impressed, not by the similarities of these writings, but by the great differences between the biblical books and these false writings.

The Scriptures are said to be "God-breathed." Neither church councils nor "words of knowledge" are said to have that authority. We return to the words of Paul: "All Scripture is God-breathed and is useful for teaching, rebuking, correcting and training in righteousness, so that the man of God may be thoroughly equipped for every good work" (2 Timothy 3:16-17).

Only a select group of books meet such a high standard.

FIVE
A SUCCESSFUL SEARCH FOR JESUS

But you told me the New Testament is based on fabrications."

Langdon smiled. "Sophie, *every* faith in the world is based on fabrication. That is the definition of *faith*—acceptance of that which we imagine to be true, that which we cannot prove."[1]

With that, the discussion in *The Da Vinci Code* turns to the supposed existence of thousands of secret documents that would give scientific evidence that the New Testament is false testimony. Surprisingly, however, Langdon is not in favor of digging up the documentation that would destroy Christianity because he does not want to upset the faith of Christians, nor for that matter those of any other religion.

He continued, "Those who truly understand their faiths understand the stories are metaphorical. . . . Religious allegory has become a part of the fabric of reality. And living in that reality helps millions of people cope and be better people."[2] In other words, the story of Jesus isn't true, but it is helpful for living in the world. As we shall see in the next chapter, this is like saying that one can enjoy leaves even though trees do not exist!

So, is it true that the New Testament is built on fabrications and that the Christian faith is only accepting what we "imagine to be true" and that

WAS JESUS A FEMINIST? DID THE CHURCH SUPPRESS THAT ASPECT OF CHRIST'S TEACHINGS?

Jesus most assuredly was not a feminist in the modern sense of the word. He *did*, however, reject those cultural norms that put women in a disrespected place as second-class citizens of the Kingdom. He countered the expectation of the rabbis by elevating women to a place of honor and influence.

which we "cannot prove"? What do we say to those who tell us that the New Testament is unreliable? How solid is the evidence for the Christian faith? Do you find your faith shaken when you read that evidence might exist somewhere that disproves the New Testament?

This chapter will answer the following questions: Is there good reason to still believe in the traditional Jesus, the Jesus of the creeds? Do recent revisions so seriously undercut the New Testament portrait of Jesus that we are free to mold him into whatever image we wish?

THE JESUS SEMINAR

Perhaps no group of scholars has done more to try to discredit the New Testament portrait of Christ than the Jesus Seminar, which meets regularly in California to vote on what they believe Christ did or did not say and do. The participants devised a creative plan on how to cast their ballots: Each person drops a plastic bead into a bucket. The color of the bead signifies the scholar's opinion. Red means "That's Jesus!" Pink: "Sure sounds like Jesus"; Gray: "Well, maybe"; Black: "There has been some mistake."

Their conclusion is that only about 18 percent of the words ascribed to Jesus in the Gospels may actually have been spoken by him. The rest of the sayings were apparently made up by the early church and put into the mouth of Jesus. Of course, the resurrection of Christ was rejected, along with all of the other miracles. We should not be surprised that they concluded that Jesus did *not* say, "I am the way, the truth, and the life: no man cometh unto the Father, but by me" (John 14:6, KJV). Only politically correct words and deeds are attributed to him.

These left-wing scholars' stated purpose is to change the way people think about Jesus. They have gone public, and national newspapers regularly report their conclusions. They want to "free the Bible from the religious right" and believe that our culture needs a new view of Jesus, a Jesus who speaks to modern concerns such as feminism, multiculturalism, ecology, and political correctness. This Jesus is a mere man.

If you believe the Bible as I do, I can assure you that we have nothing to fear from these subjective speculations. In fact, properly understood, these scholars actually strengthen our faith rather than undermine it! Indeed, such criticism of Jesus turns out to be *just one more reason to believe that Christ is who the New Testament writers claim he is!*

Let me explain.

First, keep in mind that these radical views are entirely based on the subjective hunches of each scholar; in effect, every decision is made with an unwavering bias against miracles. In the introduction to *The Five Gospels* (which includes *The Gospel of Thomas*) by Robert Funk, founder of the Jesus Seminar, the author states: "The Christ of creed and dogma who had been firmly in place in the Middle Ages, can no longer command the assent of those who have seen the heavens through Galileo's telescope."[3]

We have seen the heavens through a telescope, the argument goes, so we can no longer believe in a miraculous Christ. Remember, they are not forced to their conclusions by historical or archaeological discoveries but by prior convictions and self-consciously chosen naturalistic presuppositions. Yes, the scholars have extensively studied the life and times of Jesus, but only to try to shape their personal view of who Jesus really was: Jesus the man, the *mere* man.

No historical evidence will ever cause them to reexamine their conclusions because their naturalistic view of the world comes prior to historical investigation. Driven by a strong antisupernatural bias, they end where they begin: In their minds, there can be no supernatural Jesus.

Once Jesus is cut off from the eyewitness accounts, everyone is free to interpret him however one wishes, with as much imagination or creativity as one can muster. Jesus is made into whomever we want him to be. Speaking of the Jesus Seminar, Howard Clark Kee, a New Testament professor emeritus at Boston University, called the work of the seminar "an academic disgrace" and said that its members "seemed determined to find a Jesus free of such features embarrassing to modern intellectuals, as demons, miracles and predictions about the future."[4] We are on much firmer ground when we believe the men who were there rather than the revisionists living two thousand years after these events.

THE QUEST FOR THE HISTORICAL JESUS

The attempt to debunk the Jesus of the New Testament has a long history. For centuries liberal scholars have tried to separate the historical Jesus (Jesus the mere man) from what they call "the Christ of faith"; that is, the Christ of legend and myth. They have tried to peel away all of the miraculous sayings and works in the Gospels to find this *man,* Jesus. In the process, they have ended up with as many different "historical Jesuses" as there are scholars. Rather than writing a biography of Christ, each scholar has, in effect, written a biography of himself!

This search for the historical Jesus is a kind of Rorschach ink-blot test. Since the New Testament was deemed unbelievable and one's own conception of Jesus was all that mattered, many different portraits of Christ have emerged. Some writers pictured him as a countercultural hippie; others saw him as a Jewish reactionary, a charismatic rabbi, or even a homosexual magician. The famed humanitarian Albert Schweitzer wrote his own biography of Christ and concluded that it was Jesus' insanity that drove him to claim divinity.

The life of Christ is a mirror in which each scholar sees a reflection of his own doubts, aspirations, and agenda.

In the end, the authors reveal more about

themselves than about Jesus. Their dizzy contradictions and subjective opinions have forced many scholars to throw up their hands in exasperation and admit that the quest for the historical Jesus has ended in failure. The scholars discovered that the portrait of Christ in the New Testament is a whole piece of cloth; they were not able to find the seam in the garment that would separate "Jesus the mere man" from "Jesus the divine miracle worker." No razor blade was sharp enough to carve up the New Testament with any rational objectivity. Realizing that the search for the historical Jesus was futile, some even concluded that the best course of action is to simply say that we know nothing whatsoever about him.

Perhaps you've heard the story about Edward Burne-Jones's celebrated painting, *Love among the Ruins.* The painting was destroyed by an art firm that had been hired to restore it. Though they had been warned that it was a watercolor and therefore needed special attention, they used the wrong liquid and dissolved the paint.

Throughout the ages men have tried to reduce the bright New Testament portrait of Christ to gray tints—to sponge out the miracles, to humanize his claims. So far, however, no one has found the solvent needed to neutralize the original and reduce it to a cold, dull canvas. No matter who tries to blend its hues with those of ordinary men, the portrait remains stubborn, immune to those who seek to distinguish between the original and a supposed updated revision.

Try as they might, these unbelievers cannot find a purely human Jesus anywhere on the pages of the New Testament. Their subjectivism left them with random bits and pieces of information, but no coherent view of Jesus. They are faced with a clear choice: *Either accept him as he is portrayed in the New Testament or confess ignorance about him*. In effect, they are faced with the stark realization that the Gospel portrait is either all true or all false. Determined not to accept a miraculous Christ, some scholars have opted to say that there might not have been a historical Jesus at all!

The point is that no matter how far we try to go back to find the real Jesus, we always meet a supernatural Jesus. It is unbelief and not scholarship that forces people to say that the New Testament was built on "fabrication" and that faith "is that which we can imagine to be true."

ERWIN W. LUTZER

Augustine lived before scholars chewed up the
Scriptures according to their personal whims.
Nevertheless, even in his day some people believed
what they wanted and discarded the rest. He
wrote, "If you believe what you like in the gospels
and reject what you don't like, it's not the gospel
you believe, but yourself."

Yes!

AN EVALUATION OF NEW TESTAMENT DOCUMENTS

The best way to confirm the accuracy of the New
Testament documents is to test them with the same

DID JESUS INTEND MARY MAGDALENE TO LEAD THE CHURCH?

The evidence for this claim comes largely from the
Gospel of Mary, which was written by an unknown
author in about the second century. It affirms that
Jesus loved Mary more than the other disciples. This
account is an attempt by the Gnostics to give legitimacy to their esoteric doctrines of knowledge and to
argue that women can teach in the church. The historical reliability of this story is questionable, but
even if it were true, it says nothing about Jesus'
intention to build the church on Mary.

standards used to investigate any other historical document. John Warwick Montgomery in his book *History and Christianity,* spells out three tests that can be applied to the New Testament.[5]

First, there is the *biographical* test, which analyzes the textual tradition through which a document reaches us. This test answers the question: Since we do not have the original documents, is our present text based on reliable copies? Since there is a 250-year gap (give or take a few years) between the originals and the copies that are in existence today, can we be sure that we have a reliable textual tradition?

The answer is a resounding *yes.* Listen to the words of Sir Frederic Kenyon, former director and principal librarian of the British Museum:

In no other case is the interval of time between the composition of the book and date of the earliest extant manuscripts so short as in that of the New Testament. . . . We believe that we have in all essentials an accurate text of the seven extant [existing] plays of Sophocles; yet the earliest substantial manuscript upon which it is based was written more than 1,400 years after the poet's death. Aeschylus, Aristophanes, and Thucydides are in the same state;

while with Euripides the interval is increased to 1,600 years. For Plato it may be put at 1,300 years, for Demosthenes as low as 1,200.[6]

If you are still concerned about the gap of 250 years, remember that we can independently confirm the text of the New Testament in several ways. First, by papyri manuscripts that were discovered in Egypt. These manuscripts are dated as early as AD 125 and contain fragments of the New Testament. Second, extensive quotations of the New Testament occur in the writings of the early church fathers. This is seen as further proof that the New Testament writings were known to them, and that they possessed the same content we have today. To quote Kenyon again:

The interval, then, between the dates of the original composition and the earliest extant [existing] evidence becomes so small as to be in fact negligible, and the last foundation for any doubt that the Scriptures have come down to us substantially as they were written has now been removed. Both the authenticity and the general integrity of the books of the New Testament may be regarded as finally established.[7]

Even when we allow for the errors copyists made and take into account that the various manuscripts do have minor variations, we still have a reliable biblical text upon which our faith is based. No doctrine is affected by differences in spelling, word order, or the addition of an explanatory word or phrase.

The second test is *internal*, that is, the claims of the writers themselves. Do they claim to be eyewitnesses to the events recorded, or did they at least receive their information from credible sources? John claimed to have been an eyewitness to the events of his Gospel and explicitly says he was present at the Crucifixion (John 19:35). Luke told us that there were many accounts of the life of Christ available to him, and then he continued, "It seemed fitting for me as well, having investigated everything carefully from the beginning, to write it out for you in consecutive order, most excellent Theophilus; so that you might know the exact truth about the things you have been taught" (Luke 1:3-4, NASB).

The New Testament writers do not discredit themselves by internal contradictions or mystical ramblings. Their own moments of doubt and skepticism motivated them to search out the truth so they could write with credibility. Many of the books of the New Testament were written when people who had witnessed the events were still alive. In some instances the writers called upon others to verify that what they were writing was correct. When Paul argued for the physical resurrection of Christ, he pointed to those who were still living who could verify this claim (1 Corinthians 15:6).

Finally, there is the *external* test. Do other historical materials confirm or deny the content of the documents? Limited space forbids an appeal to archaeology, except to say that most often it confirms the writings of the Bible. Whether it is the story of Abraham, the existence of the Hittites, or the details of Solomon's reign, the Old Testament has proven time and again that its history is reliable.

As for the New Testament, each year brings more discoveries that the accounts are trustworthy. And we might add that the famous historian Josephus referred to the resurrection of Christ. "At this time there was a wise man called Jesus, and his conduct was good and he was known to be virtuous. . . . Pilate condemned him to be crucified and die. But those who had become his disciples did not abandon his discipleship. They reported that he had appeared to them three days after his crucifixion and that he was alive."[8]

COULD THE DISCIPLES HAVE MADE UP THE STORY?

Might it not have been possible—as liberal theologians suggest—that Jesus' followers made up the stories about him out of a desire to turn a mere man into the Son of God? This is, of course, the teaching of the Jesus Seminar and others who attempt to strip Jesus of his divinity.

Montgomery pointed out that this theory is simply not plausible. For one thing, Jesus would have been a poor candidate to choose for deification. His teaching contradicted the messianic expectation of the times. The Jews of the day were expecting a messiah who would come with the sword to smite the Romans and restore the land to the Jews. As S. W. Baron in his *Social and Religious History of the Jews* explained, the common consensus was that the Messiah would unite Israel and Judah against the Romans.[9] This hardly sounds like the Jesus who said, "My kingdom is not of this world" (John 18:36). As Montgomery said, "The single fact that official Jewry crucified Jesus for blasphemy is sufficient grounds for rejecting the idea that Jesus fulfilled the messianic dreams of the time!"[10]

Second, the followers of Jesus would never have declared that a man was God; such an offense was unthinkable. This would have gone against the teachings of first-century Jewish ideology. Two laws were the bedrock of the Jewish faith: (1) the unity of God and (2) the first commandment that "you shall have no other gods before me" (Exodus 20:3). To take a mere man and ascribe deity to him was sacrilege of the highest order; stoning was the punishment for such a crime.

There is only one rational reason why Jesus is portrayed in the New Testament as God: Jesus himself made such claims, and the weight of the evidence convinced the disciples that he spoke the truth. The disciples were hardheaded fishermen whose skepticism had to be overcome by a man who claimed to be the Messiah and had the miracles and wisdom to prove it!

Thomas, for example, was not about to believe in the Resurrection, even on the uniform testimony of ten men. He said, "Unless I see the nail marks in his hands and put my finger where the nails were, and put my hand into his side, I will not believe it" (John 20:25).

Jesus graciously granted his request. He came through a locked door and said, "Put your finger here; see my hands. Reach out your hand and put it into my side. Stop doubting and believe." Thomas's response? "My Lord and my God!" (John 20:26-28).

That hardly sounds like a gullible man who was willing to believe fanciful tales about a would-be messiah. The portrait of Jesus in the Gospels could not have been manufactured. Like the centurion who watched Christ die, we are compelled to add our voices to those who say, "Surely this man was the Son of God!" (Mark 15:39).

EYEWITNESS TESTIMONY

The apostle Peter, knowing that he was about to die, wanted to leave a final witness to his readers about the historicity of Jesus. So he writes, "I think it is right to refresh your memory as long as I live in the tent of this body, because I know that I will soon put it aside, as our Lord Jesus Christ has made clear to me. And I will make every effort to see that after my departure you will always be able to remember these things" (2 Peter 1:13-15). Then follows a vivid account of what he experienced when he was with Jesus.

The false teachers in Peter's day—every age has had them—were attacking the doctrine of the glorious return of Jesus. They were arguing from the uniformity of natural law that "ever since our fathers died, everything goes on as it has since the beginning of creation" (2 Peter 3:4).

Now Peter refuted them.

WE SAW THE SON'S TRANSFORMATION

Anticipating those who *dis*believe in a miraculous Jesus, Peter said, "We did not follow cleverly invented stories when we told you about the power and coming of our Lord Jesus Christ, but we were eyewitnesses of his majesty" (2 Peter 1:16). We could translate the Greek phrase, "We did not follow sophisticated myths." The apostles were not carried away by fanaticism; they were not prone to accept questionable accounts that could not be checked out.

Peter continued, "For he received honor and glory from God the Father when the voice came to him from the Majestic Glory, saying, 'This is my

Son, whom I love; with him I am well pleased'" (2 Peter 1:17). He had a right to speak, he said, for he was on the Mount of Transfiguration and saw for himself the glory and honor given to Jesus.

Peter said they did not see a miracle because they were looking for one; they were as surprised as anyone else would have been! This agrees with John's account, who also was an eyewitness to Jesus' majesty: "We have seen his glory, the glory of the One and Only, who came from the Father, full of grace and truth" (John 1:14).

So Peter, James, and John saw firsthand the glory the Son of God will have in the coming kingdom. They were not just curious men exploring the possibility of the Christian faith, but rather they were invited to see a glimpse of Jesus as he exists apart from the limitations of the flesh. They had a ringside seat to the experiences of God and knew that Jesus' promise of a coming kingdom would not die with him.

WE HEARD THE FATHER'S VOICE

Peter continued, "We ourselves heard this voice that came from heaven when we were with him on the sacred mountain" (2 Peter 1:18).

Peter says they were *eyewitnesses,* but also *ear witnesses.* Just think of the arrogance of those who believe they have a better grasp on what happened over two thousand years ago than those who were eyewitnesses of his majesty! Who are we going to believe—those with a strong antisupernatural bias, or those who were actually there and saw it all? Personally, I hope you join me in believing those who assure us that they did not follow sophisticated myths!

WE CONFIRMED THE SPIRIT'S RECORD

Peter then reminded readers that the disciples' experiences confirmed prophecy. "We have the word of the prophets made more certain, and you will do well to pay attention to it, as to a light shining in a dark place, until the day dawns and the morning star rises in your hearts" (2 Peter 1:19). Some interpret this as Peter's way of saying that prophecy is an even surer guarantee than his own report; in other words, an even stronger argument for the Second Coming is that the prophets foretold it.

These words can also be interpreted in this way: "What we saw on the Mount of Transfiguration makes it even more certain that what is foretold in

DID JESUS' FOLLOWERS INVENT THE STORY THAT JESUS IS GOD? WAS JESUS MERELY HUMAN, NOT DIVINE?

There is only one rational reason why Jesus is portrayed in the New Testament as God: Jesus himself made such claims and the weight of the evidence convinced the disciples that he spoke the truth. No matter how far we try to go back to find the "real Jesus," we always meet a *supernatural* Jesus. It is unbelief, not scholarship, that leads people to say that the Jesus of the New Testament was invented by his followers.

the prophets about the Second Coming must be true." The glory they saw on the mount is the strongest evidence that the prophets spoke the truth. Moses and Elijah also appeared. Moses represented the Law, and Elijah represented the prophets; both the Law and the prophets pointed to Christ.

Peter added, "Above all, you must understand that no prophecy of Scripture came about by the prophet's own interpretation. For prophecy never had its origin in the will of man, but men spoke from God as they were carried along by the Holy Spirit" (2 Peter 1:20-21). The mark of the false prophet in the Old Testament was that he was making up the message or confusing his own thoughts with God's thoughts (Ezekiel 13:3). The true prophet often had to proclaim what he did not want to say; he often had to bring hard messages no one would be tempted to make up.

In the end, then, Peter says the Trinity confirmed the deity of Jesus. The disciples *saw* the Son, they *heard* the Father, and they *confirmed* that the writings were inspired by the Holy Spirit. And so we are faced with a decision: Whose opinion should we believe? Should we follow those who want to debunk the politically incorrect Christ or those who were credible eyewitnesses of these first-century events? If the New Testament were built on fabrications, its credibility would have been destroyed long ago.

Consider the words of Bernard Ramm:

A thousand times over, the death knell of the Bible has been sounded, the funeral procession formed, the inscription cut on the tombstone, and the committal read. But somehow the corpse never stays put.

No other book has been so chopped, sliced, sifted, scrutinized and vilified. What book on philosophy or religion or psychology or belles letters of classical or modern times has been subject to such a mass attack as the Bible? with such venom and skepticism? with such thoroughness and erudition? upon every chapter, line and tenet?

The Bible is still loved by millions and studied by millions.[11]

Perhaps the reason for the Bible's longevity can be found, not in the men who wrote it, but in the God who inspired it. "The grass withers, the flower fades, but the word of our God stands forever" (Isaiah 40:8, NASB).

In *The Da Vinci Code,* Dan Brown said that thousands of secret documents exist that disprove Christianity. Let's call his bluff and insist that he find them and present them to the world! Of course it is a cheap shot to make such a claim without offering the tiniest shred of evidence. How desperate one must be to build a case for unbelief on imaginary documents.

We do well to bow before the Christ of the New Testament, accepting his claims and believing that his crucifixion was a sacrifice for sinners. And when we do, we have the promise, "Yet to all who received him, to those who believed in his name, he gave the right to become children of God—children born not of natural descent, nor of human decision or a husband's will, but born of God" (John 1:12-13).

SIX

Nothing in Christianity is original. The pre-Christian God Mithras—called *the Son of God* and *the Light of the World*—was born on December 25, died, was buried in a rock tomb, and then resurrected in three days."[1] This statement, made by Sir Leigh Teabing in *The Da Vinci Code,* accuses the New Testament church of "borrowing" its teachings from stories about another god who is described in pagan traditions. The clear implication of course, is that Christianity is based on mythology—*stolen* mythology at that.

We can confidently say that Christianity did not borrow its teachings about Jesus from the legends of Mithras that were popular in ancient Rome. For one thing, the Old Testament predicted the life, death, and resurrection of Jesus hundreds of years before the superstitions of Mithras surfaced. In the book of Isaiah, written about seven centuries before Christ, we find prophecies about Jesus' virgin birth (7:14), his beatings (52:14), and his crucifixion (53:1-11). In the Psalms we have a preview of his resurrection (16:10). To these we could add dozens of other predictions that Jesus' life and death fulfilled. Remarkably, the Old Testament and the New Testament fit together like a hand in a glove. As someone once said, "The New is in the Old concealed, and the Old is in the New revealed."

Numerous conflicting superstitions are associated with Mithras. This is due in large part to the fact that the followers of Mithraism did not keep written documents, choosing instead to pass on their religion through secret rituals. What we know of the movement comes from outsiders who opposed these legends.

It is generally believed that Mithras was a god of the ancient Persians as well as of the Aryans of India, who made him one of their twelve high gods. In the Zoroastrian religion, he was an angel, a god of "heavenly light." In Rome, Mithras was associated with the mystery religions and honored by the military as a god of war.

Because of these diverse views, the cult of Mithras was continually evolving, adapting itself to the needs of a particular group or culture. Understandably, this religion can be interpreted in a variety of ways, and its teachings are difficult to pin down. What seems most probable is that the specific myths about Mithras's miraculous birth and becoming a "savior god" were modeled after the stories of Jesus and developed after Christianity came to Rome in the first century.

We've already shown that the Christian faith is rooted deeply in historical fact rather than in mythology. The early church vigorously opposed paganism and went to great lengths to make sure that the church did not adopt its myths and practices. In this chapter we'll look at more evidence that supports the originality of Christianity.

Perhaps the best way for us to show that Christianity is radically different from all other religions and superstitions is to contrast it with ancient Gnosticism, which today is presented as "another way to be Christian." We will see why some readers of *The Da Vinci Code* prefer its teachings to Christianity. Although many people think that all the religions of the world are essentially the same and only superficially different, we shall see that the opposite is true: *Christianity is fundamentally different and only superficially the same as other religions and philosophies.* It is indeed an original.

PREVAILING BELIEFS

People today are clearly seeking to connect with the metaphysical world. Walk into a bookstore and you will see many shelves of books devoted to the spiritual quest. We have books and television programs that speak of spirituality and healing,

IS CHRISTIANITY JUST A REHASH OF OTHER MYTHS, LIKE THAT OF MITHRAS?

The Christian faith is deeply rooted in historical fact rather than mythology. The cult of Mithras was continually evolving and historically hard to pin down; its legends varied from one era to another and from one locale to another. What seems most probable is that the specific myths about Mithras's miraculous birth and becoming a "savior god" were modeled after the stories of Jesus.

spirituality and self-awareness, and, of course, spirituality and sex. Many paths are available, and everyone is invited to choose his or her own path to fulfillment.

Millions of people who have never heard the word *Gnosticism* are devotees of its essential teachings. To understand Gnosticism is to understand why it is so attractive to a generation that is committed to diversity and do-it-yourself spirituality. As we contrast what the Gnostics believed with the historic Christian faith, we are, in effect, giving a critique of today's religious climate.

Although Gnosticism was a very diverse movement with many complicated teachings, we will discuss its doctrine of Jesus in its most popular form. Time and space necessitates that we limit our discussion to a few of the teachings about Jesus as given in just a few of the texts. For a more serious discussion of Gnosticism, a number of excellent works are available.[2]

WHICH JESUS?

In general we can say this: The Gnostics believed that the death, burial, and resurrection of Jesus were irrelevant—they did not bring about our salvation.

What mattered to them was the immediate presence of Christ, accessible to those who experienced *gnosis*, that is, the enlightenment available to those who were awakened to it. Thus they encouraged a direct experience of God, without the mediation of Christ or the constraints of the church.

Gnostics did not view Jesus' death as an act of atonement, but rather as an occasion for discovering the divine self within.[3] Even those Gnostics who believed Jesus died on behalf of others saw his death—not as atonement—but as a means to awaken others to their own divine possibilities. As the *logos*, Jesus was able to transcend death to bring us *gnosis*. (That word *logos* was often used by Gnostics to refer to reason or a kind of special knowledge.)

As for the Resurrection, the Gnostics unanimously rejected Jesus' physical resurrection. One writer referred to it as "the faith of fools." Therefore, the Resurrection was not a unique event where one man cheated death and actually returned from the grave. Rather, the Resurrection was interpreted symbolically, as a metaphor to explain how Christ's presence could be experienced. What mattered was not seeing a physical form come back from the dead but rather experiencing a "spiritual vision." Thus, in *The Gospel of Mary,* the resurrection appearances are interpreted as appearances of visions, dreams, and trances.[4]

Although the Gnostics believed these visions were objective occurrences, the fact remains that they either denied the historicity of the New Testament Gospels or considered them unimportant. For them, the immediate experience of Christ mattered, not the events of his earthly experiences.

Christ is of help to us, but he did nothing that was indispensable for our salvation. In their mind, the life of Jesus on earth was not a necessary, one-time event in which God came to earth to rescue humanity. Jesus was to be honored but not worshipped as a divine redeemer or mediator.

SELF-SALVATION

Gnostics also believed that when we encounter God, we are in effect encountering ourselves, for knowledge of the self is knowledge of God. Thus, theology is really anthropology—we are actually lighting the spark of the divine that exists in all of us. God, however he or she is defined, is really an extension of ourselves.

In *The Gospel of Thomas,* when the disciples asked

Jesus where they should go, he replied, "There is light within a man of light, and it lights up the whole world. If he does not shine, he is darkness."[5] Thus, we are not directed to Christ who exists outside of us as a savior, but rather we must look to the light within to save ourselves.

In *The Gospel of Philip,* we discover a more radical notion of our relationship to God. There we read: "God created humanity; [but now human beings] create God. That is the way it is in the world—human beings make gods, and worship their creation. It would be appropriate for the gods to worship human beings!"[6]

According to this theory, neither Jesus nor any other religious leader is God in a unique sense. We all can be gods, and indeed, we can make our own! Man's problem, according to the Gnostics, is not sin, but ignorance; we simply need to know how to access the *gnosis* and experience our own enlightenment. Man, instead of being saved from outside himself, must come to his own rescue. People are quite free to create God according to their own image and after their own likeness.

Thus it goes without saying that we do not need to believe a given set of doctrines for salvation. Teachers might serve the limited purpose of leading us in the direction of truth, but for the ultimate experience of *gnosis* we must proceed on our own. Indeed for some Gnostics, to submit to the clerical hierarchy requires that we submit to "blind guides" whose authority comes from the malevolent creator.[7] In fact, doctrines and belief systems are actually seen as hindrances to progress along the Gnostic path.

THE GNOSTICS, THEN AND NOW

The Gnostics would likely have approved of the Parliament of the World Religions that I attended back in 1993. In all, about 6,500 delegates from all over the world convened to discuss the possibility of unifying the religions of the world. The basic premises were these:

- No one religion is superior to another.
- Doctrines should be viewed as subjective paths that need revision rather than as inflexible truths.
- Proselytizing should be forbidden, because trying to persuade others to believe in a particular religion only raises the specter of exclusivity and the dreaded word *superiority*.

- The most important pursuit is one that seeks a religious experience defined according to personal taste and inclination.

Gnostics would agree that the path we take does not matter as long as we experience our own *gnosis*—the mystical center where enlightenment is experienced.

At the Parliament I met people who said, "I'm a Christian Buddhist" or "I'm into New Age Christianity." People spoke about taking the best from the religious smorgasbord and creating their own particular combination and preference of beliefs. In many of the sessions, Jesus was damned with faint praise. Some said he was important for the West but not the East. Others said he was a great teacher and even a unique revelation from God— but only one of a number of such revelations.

Gnosticism is making a comeback in Christian circles because it is so in sync with our overwhelming move toward religious diversity, an attitude that insists the path to the divine cannot be well-defined. In this view, no one has the right to say, "This is the wrong path!" Authority resides within each individual and should not be imposed upon

IS GNOSTICISM ANOTHER VERSION OF CHRISTIANITY?

The Gnostic Jesus and the Jesus of the New Testament are radically different. Far from being the authentic version of Christianity, Gnosticism was a parasite that attempted to tie its platonic ideas to the fledgling, but popular, Christian movement. Christianity is a historical religion, rooted in certain verifiable facts, while Gnosticism is a theory of ideas that is not grounded in space or time events.

that individual by anyone, including Jesus. In other words, it's perfectly acceptable to have mystical experiences that are in no way tied to salient events in the life of the historical Jesus.

Recently I listened to a talk show where a medium who claimed to communicate with the dead was the guest. When asked whether there was a judgment after death, he said, "No, when we die, we judge ourselves." If the Gnostics had believed in the final judgment (most did not), they most assuredly would have agreed with that sentiment. If we can save ourselves, we can judge ourselves too.

So if people are seeking God in their own way

and if there is some truth in every religion, why talk about Jesus as if he is the only reasonable option? I've had people tell me that if Jesus works for me, fine; but if something or someone else works better for another, that is fine too. Why not be tolerant and accepting of the options available in our diverse culture?

THE GREAT DIVIDE

So how is Christianity different from the myths of Mithras and the mysticism of the Gnostics? How can we be sure we have an original, not a copy of some other faith? Of course, it is possible for people of various beliefs to have a religious experience of sorts—but on our own, we are like ants on a Rembrandt painting, noticing the roughness of the canvas and the changing colors beneath our feet, but incapable of understanding what we are seeing. God's revelation in the New Testament will help us find the way.

We begin by noting that Christianity parts with other religious beliefs in its understanding of sin. Far from believing that God is essentially like us, Christians understand the Bible's clear teaching that we have transgressed God's laws and are not capable of returning to fellowship with our Creator on our own. This doctrine of original sin (and our resultant sinful behavior) resonates deeply with our own experience. No one reading these pages has escaped the pain of injustice, the stifling effects of selfishness, and the deep pangs of regret.

I think it was G. K. Chesterton who said that he couldn't understand why anyone would deny original sin, since it was the only doctrine that could be proved by reading the daily newspaper! We read of the evil others have done, and if we are honest, we know intuitively that we are capable of essentially the same acts. We also know intuitively that we are accountable to someone beyond ourselves. Guilt is not a feeling that can be unlearned. The guilty conscience points to an inner awareness that we have violated our own standards and that someday we shall be called to account by One who knows the secrets of our own soul.

Combine this with the biblical teaching of the holiness of God. He is presented in Scripture as being pure, sinless, and without defect. He is the personal Creator, Sustainer, and Judge to whom we must give account. The Bible rejects the notion that we can call ourselves God, acting as though

ERWIN W. LUTZER

we have the marks of divinity; indeed this was the first lie of the demonic religion of Genesis 3. To be sure, we are creatures created in God's image, but in essence we are forever unlike him.

Enter Jesus.

Jesus is the only one who has the qualifications of a Savior; that is, the ability to repair the breach between us and the God of the Bible. Jesus is able to tell us what God is like, what he expects of us, and the terms under which he is willing to connect with us. In short, in Jesus we find someone with inside information, someone who is able to speak on God's behalf. Thanks to Jesus, we can have a faith that fits our need—exactly. In him we find a redeeming God.

To put it simply, Jesus insisted that his entry into this world was a onetime, nonrepeatable, historical event in which salvation was purchased for those who would trust him. He had to be physically present for this act of atonement to be made—as physically present as those firefighters who rescued people in the 9/11 tragedy in New York. Teachings and wonderful ideas cannot rescue a person from a burning building.

Although a mere man can rescue another human from an enflamed building, only a divine man can reconcile us to God. So only the divine/human Jesus can bring us to the presence of the God whose justice we have offended. This Jesus needed to be born as a man, die, and make sacrifice for our sins, a sacrifice that was received by the Father during the six hours that this God-man hung on the cross.

Our offenses are as real as a thief who steals money from a bank vault. And as restitution demands that the money be replaced, so the payment for our sin had to be made before we could be reconciled to God. Ideas cannot bridge the gap between us and God; only an act of atonement can.

I do not mean, of course, that the payment Jesus made on the cross was some physical entity, such as a wad of hundred-dollar bills. But we do read, "For you know that it was not with perishable things such as silver or gold that you were redeemed from the empty way of life handed down to you from your forefathers, but with the precious blood of Christ, a lamb without blemish or defect" (1 Peter 1:18-19). Jesus had to die; blood had to be shed; sin had to be borne; the Father's justice had to be satisfied.

Let the pagans, ancient or modern, borrow what they wish from the sayings of Jesus, but if they deny that his death and resurrection were the central focus of his mission, they are denying what it means to be a Christian. Reduce Jesus' impact to his teachings alone, and you cut the heart out of what the New Testament repeatedly calls the gospel: the Good News.

It was this dogged insistence that Christianity was tied to the historicity of Jesus that made Paul argue that the physical resurrection could be verified by the five hundred who actually saw Jesus and that many of these witnesses were still living. Then he adds, "And if Christ has not been raised, your faith is futile; you are still in your sins" (1 Corinthians 15:17).

The Incarnation is the great divide between Christianity and Gnosticism, and for that matter between Christianity and Islam. In the Islamic faith, the Incarnation is the greatest blasphemy—Muslims believe that Allah can have no direct contact with the world. In contrast, Christianity teaches that we are not saved by Christ's example or his ideas; nor are we saved if we have a revelation or vision of him. Our own *gnosis*—no matter how wonderfully contrived and experienced—cannot remove the objective barrier that our sin has caused between our God and us.

This explains why the early Christian writers refused to mix Christianity and other religions. They most assuredly were not inclined to "borrow" anything from pagan faiths, standing strongly in opposition to them. While other religions may have similar ethical teachings to Christianity, they differ at the central issue: the Incarnation and what it has accomplished.

All forms of spirituality that say we can reach God (however defined) on our own stand in stark opposition to the salvation event of God through Christ. This infinite and unbridgeable chasm pits Gnosticism against Christianity with no hope of reaching a halfway compromise. Only those who misunderstand the true nature of Christianity can call Gnosticism "an alternate way to be Christian."

The Good News of the New Testament is that God has given us the ministry of reconciliation "that God was reconciling the world to himself in Christ, not counting men's sins against them" (2 Corinthians 5:19). Christianity asserts that it was the Incarnation and the subsequent earthly acts of Jesus that are God's saving event in the world.

GOD, YES—BUT WHY JESUS?

We often hear, "I'm into God, but not Jesus," as if there are many ways to access the divine. The Bible has two warnings for us. First, it warns against re-making God according to our own liking: "You shall have no other gods before me" (Exodus 20:3), the first commandment. The words were freshly chiseled on Moses' tablet of stone when the Israelites already violated the commandment by fashioning the golden calf. We also commit idolatry when we fashion a god according to our own understanding.

But there is a second warning: We must come to the right God in the *right way*. Cain and Abel both came to the right God, but one brought an offering that was accepted while the other's was rejected. The New Testament speaks of those who have "gone in the way of Cain" (Jude 1:11, KJV); that is, those who think they can come to God in their own way and on their own terms.

Nadab and Abihu were Aaron's sons and

Moses' nephews. They were consecrated to God, like seminary students of the day training for full-time ministry. One day they offered to the Lord "unauthorized fire," and God replied in kind: "So fire came out from the presence of the Lord and consumed them, and they died before the Lord" (Leviticus 10:2).

We are tempted to charge God with overreacting. These were young men who deserved a second chance; furthermore, they were the sons of Aaron, the high priest. We would expect a bit of leeway. But right there at the altar of God, Nadab and Abihu faced immediate annihilation—no trial, no second chance.

Why did God do this? He himself explained: "Among those who approach me I will show myself holy; in the sight of all the people I will be honored" (Leviticus 10:3). The mistake of these men was not that they came to the wrong God but that they came in the wrong way. They learned the hard way that *not just any way will do*.

All access to God's presence must be mediated; we as sinners cannot simply approach him on our own. Why must we come through Jesus? *As the God-man, Jesus is perfectly sinless and therefore the only one qualified to give us the righteousness by which we can stand in God's holy presence.*

Christianity stands in unbending opposition to any form of the notion that salvation involves our own effort. All human merit—those deeds that make us feel better about ourselves—had to be permanently set aside in order for us to be reconciled with God. Deeds of compassion and kindness are found in all religions of the world; obviously it is much better to be a good person than a bad person. But Christianity asserts that none of these works is capable of changing God's mind about our sin.

We like to think of ourselves as better than others. But when we compare ourselves to God— which is the only standard he accepts—we realize that there is little difference among those of us in the human family. We have nothing in common with the holiness of God. As Augustine said, "He who understands the holiness of God, despairs in trying to appease him." If God did not take the initiative to save us, we could not be saved.

How can God associate with sinners and still maintain his honor? God's holiness could not be tainted nor compromised to achieve his desired result. *It follows that only God could meet his own require-*

ments, and in Christ he did just that. No other religion lays claim to an exclusive creator God who becomes a man in order to redeem us. In these essential matters, Christianity is exclusively original.

Understandably, when Thomas asked Jesus, "How can we know the way?" he received this clear answer: "I am the way and the truth and the life. No one comes to the Father except through me" (John 14:6). A tourist walking across a desert asked a guide, "Where is the path?" to which the guide replied, "I am the path."

Someone has said that Christ is the way from the place of men's ruin all the way to God the Father, all the way from the city of destruction to the heavenly city.

When Philip requested that Jesus "show us the Father and that will be enough for us," Jesus responded simply: "Anyone who has seen me has seen the Father" (John 14:8-9). It was God who entered a simple Jewish home, God who was not ashamed to do man's work, God who knew what it was like to be tempted. It was God who hung on the cross.

In effect, Jesus said to Philip, "Listen to me! Look at me! Believe in me! Then you shall know the Father. I am able to bring you all the way home."

THE THEOLOGY OF THE CHESHIRE CAT

Religious liberals—particularly ministers—struggle with what to say at Christmas and Easter. The narratives of the New Testament stare them in the face, but if they don't believe in angels, guiding stars, or the resurrection of Jesus, what can they say with integrity? No wonder that one Easter marquee at a California church read "Easter is a time for flowers."

This past Christmas, a Chicago minister told his large congregation, "What do we do with the account of the shepherds, stars, and wise men. . . . Do we have to believe that these events happened? No, we do not have to. What matters is the *spirit* of Christmas!" So although the events supposedly didn't happen, we are invited to search for the spirit of Christmas or the spirit of Easter. The Gnostics would have loved it!

More than sixty years ago, H. Richard Neibuhr gave a description of American Christianity that is even more true today: "A God without wrath brought men without sin into a kingdom without judgment through the ministrations of a Christ without a Cross."

I'm reminded of the Cheshire cat in *Alice of Wonderland*. Remember that although the cat disappeared, his smile could still be seen in the darkness. My point, of course, is that the "spirit" of Christmas or Easter means nothing unless the events actually happened. It is like saying that we can have oranges without trees or a wheel without a center. Clearly, if these salvation events did not happen, we must save ourselves as best we can.

In describing the false teachers of his day, Jude wrote, "They are clouds without rain, blown along by the wind; autumn trees, without fruit and uprooted—twice dead. They are wild waves of the sea, foaming up their shame; wandering stars, for whom blackest darkness has been reserved forever" (Jude 1:12-13). He goes on to say what is quite obvious—namely, that these teachers "follow their own evil desires" (1:16).

Mithras is not Jesus; nor is the Jesus of the Gnostics the Jesus of Christianity. The Jesus of the New Testament was born of a virgin, died for our sins, and rose again, and he now invites us to participate in his victory. If we refuse the light, how great is the darkness!

When Jesus spoke again to the people, he said, "I am the light of the world. Whoever follows me will never walk in darkness, but will have the light of life." JOHN 8:12

AFTERWORD
FROM MY HEART TO YOURS

I once read that Swedish film director Ingmar Bergman dreamed that he was standing in a great cathedral in Europe, looking at a painting of Jesus. Desperate to hear a word from outside his own world, he whispered, "Speak to me!"

Dead silence.

That response, we are told, was the motivation for his movie *Silence*, which portrayed people who despaired of finding God. In our world, it is believed, we can only hear ourselves. No voice from outside the human predicament comes to us to tell us about ultimate reality. When seeking a word from God, we are often confronted with complete stillness.

Has God spoken, or is the universe silent regarding ultimate questions? If God has not spoken then we ourselves must be silent, for if God has not spoken, we have no insight into the meaning of life. Nor can we judge moral issues or speculate on the possibility of life beyond the grave. We must also be silent in our quest for justice, for if there is no God, we have no assurance that the scales of justice will ever be balanced.

The good news is that we have overwhelming evidence that God has spoken, and he has spoken plainly. The Bible teaches that God has spoken in nature. But nature does not tell us whether God loves the world, nor does nature tell us how we can be reconciled to our Creator.

When God wanted to speak a human language, he came to us in the person of Jesus. We read, "In the past God spoke to our forefathers through the prophets at many times and in various ways, but in these last days he has spoken to us by his Son, whom he appointed heir of all things, and through whom he made the universe" (Hebrews 1:1-2).

When Christ appeared in human form, there was an explosion of revelation. He is God's final and most complete message to mankind. And if we are honest, we must admit that the evidence for his being the Son of God is overwhelming.

At a Bible study I once attended, I met a Jewish woman who shared with me how desperately she wanted to find the truth about God. She told how she had prayed every day that God would show her how she could have a personal relationship with him. But the very thought that Christ might be the Son of God—the Messiah—frightened her. *O God,* she often prayed, *please be anyone but Jesus!*

At the end of her search, however, this woman said her worst fear came to pass: *God turned out to be Jesus!* We have many good reasons to believe she was right. Lenin claimed that if Communism was implemented there would be bread in every household, but he could never say, "I am the bread of life. He who comes to me will never go hungry, and he who believes in me will never be thirsty" (John 6:35).

Buddha taught enlightenment, yet he died seeking more light. He never said, "I am the light of the world. Whoever follows me will never walk in darkness, but will have the light of life" (John 8:12). Sigmund Freud believed that psychotherapy would heal emotional and spiritual pains. But he could not say, "Peace I leave with you; my peace I give you. I do not give to you as the world gives. Do not let your hearts be troubled and do not be afraid" (John 14:27).

Whenever I meet an atheist or an agnostic, I challenge him to a twenty-one-day experiment. Simply put, I ask him to read one chapter from the Gospel of John each day with an open mind. In fact, I even challenge unbelievers to pray, *God, if you exist, show me*. Those who have had the courage to take me up on my suggestion ruefully admit that the stories of Jesus could not have been manufactured. To believe that the same One who gave the Sermon on the Mount would deceive us about his identity just doesn't make sense. We must either recognize that he is the Son of God or explain him away as a delusional fanatic.

Years ago, I saw Rembrandt's famous painting *The Nightwatch* at the Rijksmuseum in Amsterdam. If I had suggested to the tour guide that the painting should be redone to conform to my expectations and tastes, she would have had every right to say, "This painting is not on trial—*you are*!"

Just as amateurs are quick to pronounce their verdict when beholding a masterpiece, so people today make superficial judgments about Jesus. If they would only pause a bit longer, they would realize that they, not Jesus, will be judged.

No other religion in the world teaches what Christ did: Our reconciliation to God must be a free gift to us as undeserving sinners. The reason? We do not have the kind of righteousness that God accepts; *we can't make ourselves good enough for God.* Since we can't rectify our relationship with God, we need a heavy dose of grace.

There is hope for all, even for those who believe they're beyond hope. God can save big sinners just as well as "better" ones. At issue is not the greatness of our sin, but rather the beauty of the righteousness credited to our account. Visualize a messy trail with ugly ruts; beside it runs a well-traveled road that is attractive and neat. When two feet of snow falls, you can't tell the difference between the two paths! Just so, when we trust Christ, he covers our "mess" (whether big or small) with his forgiveness and grace.

Obviously, this grace must be a free gift—free because we cannot add to it by our own goodness and promises of reform. "For it is by grace you have been saved, through faith—and this not from yourselves, it is the gift of God—not by works, so that no one can boast" (Ephesians 2:8-9).

As I close this book, I invite you to bow before Christ—not the Christ of *The Da Vinci Code* but the Christ of the New Testament, who invites all to come to him for grace and forgiveness. To a paralytic he said, "Son, your sins are forgiven" (Mark 2:5), and to an immoral woman he gave this comfort: "Your faith has saved you; go in peace" (Luke 7:50).

After his resurrection and exaltation into heaven Jesus affirmed, "Do not be afraid. I am the First and the Last. I am the Living One; I was dead, and behold I am alive for ever and ever! And I hold the keys of death and Hades" (Revelation 1:17-18).

Those are words of a Savior worth trusting!

DA VINCI DIDN'T CONVINCE ME

A mega-best-selling book and a blockbuster 2006 motion picture have millions of people asking: What's the truth behind *The Da Vinci Code*?

Tyndale House Publishers has an arsenal of solid resources to equip you with the full truth about the accuracy of the Bible, Jesus' attitude toward women, and the story of Mary Magdalene.

Mass Paperback $6.99
ISBN-13: 978-1-4143-0633-9
ISBN-10:1-4143-0633-4

Hardcover $14.99
ISBN-13: 978-0-8423-8430-8
ISBN-10: 0-8423-8430-8

THE DA VINCI DECEPTION
Dr. Erwin Lutzer
A renowned expert's comprehensive, easy-to-read explanation of the truth behind the myths

Mass Paperback $5.99
ISBN-13: 978-1-4143-0279-9
ISBN-10: 1-4143-0279-7

THE DA VINCI CODE: FACT OR FICTION?
Hank Hanegraaff, Paul Maier
Solid truth presented in convenient question-and-answer format

Hardcover $14.99
ISBN-13: 978-0-8423-8426-1
ISBN-10: 0-8423-8426-X

JESUS, LOVER OF A WOMAN'S SOUL
Dr. Erwin Lutzer, Rebecca Lutzer
The truth behind Jesus' relationships with and attitudes toward women, as seen through the eyes of those who knew him

Softcover $13.99
ISBN-13: 978-1-4143-1028-2
ISBN-10: 1-4143-1028-5

MAGDALENE
Angela Elwell Hunt
A captivating, biblically based portrayal of the controversial life of Mary Magdalene

Softcover $9.99
ISBN-13: 978-1-4143-0978-1
ISBN-10: 1-4143-0978-3

MAGGIE'S STORY
Dandi Daley Mackall
A contemporary fable that brings the story of Mary Magdalene to life for readers ages 15–19

For more information, visit http://www.davincideception.com

MILLIONS HAVE READ *THE DA VINCI CODE*.
MILLIONS MORE WILL SEE THE MOTION PICTURE.

WANT TO BE READY TO SHARE THE TRUTH?

THE DA VINCI DECEPTION EXPERIENCE

A fascinating 7-week multimedia event that will equip you
and your community to defend the truth about Jesus Christ

The Da Vinci Deception Experience contains everything you need for an
effective outreach experience that will prepare your church, youth
group, Bible study, or group of friends to respond to the questions
that millions will be asking: Who is Jesus Christ? Can I really trust
the church?

It starts with an energetic, fast-paced kickoff. In six follow-up
sessions, participants use their own copies of *The Da Vinci Deception* as
a guidebook to dig deeper into church history, the claims that Jesus
made about himself, and the legends that rose up around him.

It's turnkey: Everything you need to run this event is packaged
in one book.

The DVD-ROM includes
* Fast-paced, 20-minute kickoff video
* Six 5-minute teaching videos—one for each session
* Flyers, bulletin inserts, and other promotional resources

The workbook includes
* Fully scripted talking points for the event leader
* Questions for facilitated breakout sessions
* Tear-out worksheets and fact sheets for participants

ISBN-13: 978-1-4143-1178-4 ///// ISBN-10: 1-4143-1178-8

Purchase *The Da Vinci Code Experience* wherever Christian books are sold
or contact Tyndale House Publishers:
http://www.tyndale.com
(800) 323-9400

DISCUSSION STARTERS

For a discussion leader's guide, visit

ChristianBookGuides.com

Preface

The Da Vinci Code is a work of fiction. Why are people taking its claims so seriously?

What is the harm in a fiction book like *The Da Vinci Code*?

Do you believe that the author, Dan Brown, has an agenda in writing this novel? If so, what is it?

What might be some clues that the author has crossed the line between a purely fictional story and a propaganda piece?

How likely is it that orthodox Christian theology is merely a sinister hoax perpetrated on innocent people?

Why do you think some people are attracted to conspiracy theories?

Chapter 1: Christianity, a Politician, and a Creed

Before Constantine's conversion to Christianity, what was life in Rome like for Christians?

Constantine is credited with making Rome safe for Christians as a result of converting to Christianity himself. What were the circumstances of his conversion?

Why did Constantine convene the Council of Nicaea?

What effect were various doctrinal disputes having on Constantinople in Constantine's day?

What heresies did the Council of Nicaea address?

What arguments were made against these theories?

Why is it unlikely that Christ's divinity was "invented" at the Council of Nicaea?

How did the biblical canon come to be chosen? Was it a function of the Council of Nicaea?

What philosophies were the church leaders supposedly promoting, according to *The Da Vinci Code*?

Erwin Lutzer states that the Romans were "tolerant of everyone except those who were intolerant" (see page 22). Do you find this attitude to be in evidence today? How so?

Chapter 2: That Other Bible

What is *The Gnostic Bible*, and what is its attraction for readers?

How does the Gnostic version of Christianity differ from the Christianity of the Bible?

Is *The Gnostic Bible* as reliable as the Bible?

What did the Gnostics believe?

Why are those beliefs so popular today?

Chapter 3: Jesus, Mary Magdalene, and the Search for the Holy Grail

What is the Priory of Sion, of which Leonardo Da Vinci was purported to be a member?

According to *The Da Vinci Code*, how did Da Vinci supposedly carry out the work of the Priory?

What is the biblical evidence that Mary Magdalene was a harlot?

Was Jesus a feminist?

What evidence does *The Da Vinci Code* use to support a marriage between Jesus and Mary Magdalene? Is this evidence credible? Why or why not?

What reasons are there that Jesus could not have been married?

Chapter 4: Banned from the Bible: Why?

Why were some books included in the biblical canon and others rejected?

How is it possible that a fallible church could choose an infallible set of books for the New Testament?

Chapter 5: A Successful Search for Jesus

How can we respond to people who tell us that the New Testament is unreliable?

What is the purpose of the Jesus Seminar?

Why do the Jesus Seminar scholars have such a hard time believing that Jesus is divine?

Augustine wrote, "If you believe what you like in the gospels and reject what you don't like, it's not the gospel you believe, but yourself" (page 110). Is this statement valid in our culture as well as in Augustine's time?

What are three tests that can be applied to verify the historical accuracy of the New Testament?

Chapter 6: Divergent Paths: The Church and Its Competitors

What can we say to someone who thinks that all religions are the same?

Why is our culture so attracted to Gnosticism and its teaching?

What are some ways that Christian beliefs are different from other religions?

What can we say to someone who says, "I'm into God, but not Jesus"?

What advice would you have for someone who is considering reading *The Da Vinci Code*? How would you respond to the statement, "It's only fiction"?

ENDNOTES

Preface

1 Dan Brown, *The Da Vinci Code* (New York: Doubleday, 2003), 308.
2 Ibid., 309.
3 Ibid., 125.

Chapter One

1 Brown, *The Da Vinci Code*, 233.
2 Ibid., 231.
3 Ibid., 124.
4 Mark A. Noll, *Turning Points: Decisive Moments in the History of Christianity* (Grand Rapids: Baker Book House, 1997), 50.
5 Ibid., 51.
6 William E. Hordern, *A Layman's Guide to Protestant Theology* (New York: Macmillan, 1955), 15–16.
7 Reinhold Seeberg, *The History of Doctrine* (Grand Rapids: Baker Book House, 1964), 211.

8 E. H. Klotsche, *The History of Doctrine* (Grand Rapids: Baker Book House, 1979), 18.

9 Geoffrey Bromiley, *Historical Theology: An Introduction* (Grand Rapids: Wm. B. Eerdmans Pub. Co., 1978), 4.

10 Seeberg, *History of Doctrine,* 69.

11 Bromiley, *Historical Theology,* 14.

12 Ibid., 20.

13 Lynn Picknett and Clive Prince, *The Templar Revelation: Secret Guardians of the True Identity of Christ* (New York: Touchstone Books, Simon & Schuster, 1998), 261.

14 See http://www.tertullian.org.

15 Ibid.

16 Ibid.

Chapter Two

1 Willis Barnstone and Marvin Meyer, *The Gnostic Bible* (Boston and London: Shambhala, 2003), 19. Other translations of the *Gnostic Gospels* are also available, such as *The Nag Hammadi Library*, 3rd ed., ed. James M. Robinson (Leiden: E. J. Brill, 1988).

2 Brown, *The Da Vinci Code,* 244.

3 David Van Biema, "The Lost Gospels," *Time,* December 22, 2003, 56.

4 Ibid.

5 Ibid.

6 *Banned from the Bible,* History Channel special December 25, 2003.

7 *The Gnostic Bible,* 259.

8 Ibid., 478.

9 These three quotations are taken from *The Gospel of Thomas* as quoted in *The Gnostic Bible,* 46, 51, 57.

10 This comment from Traian Stoianovich is quoted in *The Death of Truth*, ed. Dennis McCallum (Minneapolis: Bethany House, 1996), 139.

11 Brown, *The Da Vinci Code*, 256.

12 Raymond E. Brown, "The Gnostic Gospels," *The New York Times Book Review*, January 20, 1980, 3.

13 Andrew Greeley, "Da Vinci Is More Fantasy Than Fact" book review, *National Catholic Reporter*, October 3, 2003.

14 Sir William Ramsey, *The Bearing of Recent Discovery on the Trustworthiness of the New Testament*, reprint ed. (Grand Rapids: Baker Book House, 1953), 81.

15 Van Biema, "The Lost Gospels," 56.

16 Ibid., 57.

17 Ibid.

Chapter Three

1 Brown, *The Da Vinci Code*, 245.

2 Ibid., 238.

3 Bard Thompson, *Humanists and Reformers* (Grand Rapids: Eerdmans, 1996), 141–143.

4 Bruce Boucher, "Does 'The Da Vinci Code' Crack Leonardo?" *New York Times*, Arts and Leisure, August 2, 2003.

5 Patrick R. Reardon, "'The Da Vinci Code' Unscrambled" *Chicago Tribune*, February 5, 2004, section 5, p. 4.

6 Brown, *The Da Vinci Code*, 454.

7 Barnstone and Meyer, *The Gnostic Bible*, 273.

8 Brown, *The Da Vinci Code*, 246.

9 Barnstone and Meyer, *The Gnostic Bible*, 270.

10 Ibid., 286.

11 Ibid., 479–481.

12 Picknett and Prince, *The Templar Revelation,* 350.

13 Ibid., 258.

Chapter Four

1 Brown, *The Da Vinci Code,* 231.

2 For evidence about the reliability of the Bible, read *Seven Reasons Why You Can Trust the Bible* (Chicago: Moody Press, 1998) by Erwin Lutzer.

3 D. A. Carson, Douglas Moo, and Leon Morris, *An Introduction to the New Testament* (Grand Rapids: Zondervan Publishing, 1992), 491.

4 F. F. Bruce, *The Canon of Scripture* (Downers Grove, Ill.: InterVarsity Press, 1988), 160.

5 Ibid., 204.

6 Carson, Moo, and Morris, *An Introduction to the New Testament,* 492–495.

7 Norman Geisler and William E. Nix, *A General Introduction to the Bible* (Chicago: Moody Press, 1986), 430.

8 As quoted by Don Kistler, ed., *Sola Scriptura! The Protestant Position on the Bible* (Morgan, Penn.: Soli Deo Gloria Publications, 1995), 19.

Chapter Five

1 Brown, *The Da Vinci Code,* 341.

2 Ibid., 342.

3 Robert W. Funk, Roy W. Hoover, and the Jesus Seminar, *The Five Gospels: What Did Jesus Really Say?* (New York: Scribner, 1993), 2.

4 *U.S. News & World Report,* July 1, 1991, 58.

5 John Warwick Montgomery, *History and Christianity* (Downers Grove, Ill.: InterVarsity Press, 1971).

6 Ibid., 26, 27.

7 Ibid., 28.

8 Josephus, *The Essential Writings,* ed. Paul Maier (Grand Rapids: Kregel, 1988), 264.

9 S. W. Baron, *Social and Religious History of the Jews II,* 2nd ed. (New York: Columbia University Press, 1952), 58ff. Quoted in Montgomery, 68.

10 Montgomery, *History and Christianity,* 68–69.

11 Bernard Ramm, *Protestant Christian Evidences* (Chicago: Moody Press, 1957), 232–233.

Chapter Six

1 Brown, *The Da Vinci Code,* 232.

2 Edwin M. Yamauchi, *Pre-Christian Gnosticism: A Survey of the Proposed Evidences* (Grand Rapids: Eerdmans, 1973). This excellent book surveys early Gnosticism and its relationship to the Christian church.

3 Elaine Pagels, *The Gnostic Gospels* (New York: Random House, 1979), 95.

4 Ibid., 11.

5 Ibid., 120.

6 Ibid., 122.

7 Ibid., 110–111.